I0457897

THE CORONER'S LIE

a memoir by

Mickey Murphy

Legacy Book Press LLC
Camanche, Iowa

For Dorothy Jean

Table of Contents

Prologue 1

1. French Twist...3

2. To the Lake..16

3. Big Fish Lake...26

4. The Boulevard..54

5. Mups and Mom and Gramps.....................................81

6. The Furies 96

7. The Funeral 112

8. The Aftermath 133

9. Facing the Demons 160

10. Perfect Manhattans..178

Epilogue: A Reverie 193

Acknowledgements..197

About the Author...199

No one ever keeps a secret
so well as a child.

—Victor Hugo

Prologue

I always wanted my mother's death story to be constructed out of something more than the images of what I saw, and heard, and did nothing to stop. I wanted to share it with my two sisters. I tried making my own story, starting where hers ended, cutting away the seams of that night.

Dr. DeHaan, I whisper into the phone. Dr. DeHaan? My teeth chatter violently each time I relax my jaw to speak. I glance at the clock above the stove in our kitchen. It's four o'clock in the morning. I have dialed our next door neighbor. My father has awakened me with his breath of stale liquor. He has instructed me to make this call. "Something's wrong," he says. "Something is wrong with your mother. Call the doctor and pray. If you have never prayed before, pray now."

SNIP

My father and I have already conversed once this night. But I don't tell Dr. DeHaan or my sisters. I don't tell them that I heard her say, "Don't hurt me." I don't tell them that my lip is swollen from hitting it hard on the doorjamb when I squeezed my voice across the carpet to where I thought my mother was lying. I don't tell my sisters that I tried not to wake them when I said, "Leave her alone!"

Later, I wondered, what was it about my father that made me say that? "Leave her alone!" What was he doing? What did I know?

What had I forgotten? What was it that I couldn't remember? Or wouldn't...shouldn't?

SNIP

I wonder if I have dialed yet. I hear nothing on the other end of the line. I think I've lost time somewhere, a million minutes locked in prayer. My hand is white and cold when I open the side door and let the doctor slip in. I am still clutching the phone and the plastic cord is beginning to tear along its coil. Snow is on his black bag. He pries my hand from the phone and puts it back into its cradle. I feel soothed for a moment.

The hallway seems interminably long as the doctor and I walk its length. I slide my hand along the wall to keep upright and my breath repeats itself in staccato. I turn and look into the living room where a blanket lies next to the couch. My father's glasses are on a side table. I wonder how he can see. Maybe he has made some kind of mistake.

"Where he slept last night," I murmur as if it is an alibi, and I stop at my bedroom to watch the doctor continue down the hall, making sure he doesn't slip on the carpet of my words from the night before.

SNIP

The secret haunts me. I think of that night. Frequently. More than twice a week. Each day. Every hour. Like a novena. It breaks through my rhymes and mind chatter. It smiles across the chasm that has developed between my father and me.

SNIP

SNIP SNIP SNIP SNIP SNIP

SNIP

Chapter 1

French Twist

The brevity of my mother's obituary was astonishing. It was as abrupt as the word *suddenly* which occurred in the first line, right after her name, Dorothy Donnelly. A loving wife to Thomas, a beloved mother to three girls, a fond daughter of Ray and Florine, a sister three times over, tethered to that one word—*suddenly*—to which my memories of her succumbed.

Where was the history of her thirty-seven years? Why does her narrative continue to be like a parched arroyo until the end, until her death, until the flash flood of *that night*? I wonder if the current of guilt against which I swim, even now, will ever subside. I am fearful that her death is all that will define her, and me.

My memory becomes more productive, if not safer when I think of places. The ones we shared. An indirect route, to her, a roundabout. Big Fish Lake. Hawthorne Boulevard. Saint Michael's School. They are rich with her presence. It's as if my brain can't get enough. Not about her of course, but details about everything which amount to nothing, because they aren't about her. The death, so unexpected, so, well, you know, *sudden*—it is as if she vanished during the early morning hours of my birth, severing my beloved mother-line like a guillotine. Thirteen years of lifeblood had pulsed between us and then, abruptly, (but not without ceremony!) evaporated. Memories, about us, ceased to exist. Just like her.

But her hair! That luxurious feeling of silk and slipperiness has indelibly marked each of my fingers. I am grateful for this memory of my sisters and me perched on the edge of the backseat of our Chevy, arranging and rearranging her coiffure with the deepest affection. We would be on our annual summer trek to Big Fish Lake, twelve hours from Wheaton, a suburb of Chicago, to Minnesota—plenty of time to brush through the shiny layers, coaxing waves into impossible contortions with pins and elastics. The breeze from her open window often threatened ruin to our concoctions, whipping hair into a frenzy which spilled around her face. There was nothing contrived about her appearance then, and she didn't complain as three pairs of little girl hands sporadically caressed her through the course of the long day. She looked impossibly beautiful, natural, her skin shiny with good health.

Like a lover, I would surreptitiously stare at her profile, and close one eye to trace its outline, my finger gliding in air, past her deep-set gray-green eyes, to her red lips. She had sad eyes, slanted downward at the corners just a bit, unless she smiled which created a tug of war between her brow and temple. The skin under her lower lashes was permanently smudged dark, and later, when I was older, I imagined she looked sultry rather than tired. Her eyes were rimmed with dark, short lashes, crimped upward with her Maybelline lash curler and mascaraed black, except for the month or so after she received an enormous aquamarine dinner ring from my father. It was only then that she colored her lashes a sky blue.

Sometimes I would accidentally brush my hand across her cheek to feel her flawless skin, as silky as her hair, and caress the pale blue veins in her hands where they would lie across the seat, turning her diamond around and around, catching the sun until its brilliance exploded like confetti over the family. And then, at last, perhaps saturated with touch, she would turn forward, tucking errant strands of brunette behind an ear.

She changed her hairstyle every couple of years as did my father his Chevrolet. The more mature she became (thirty!), her hair followed suit, accommodating upswept dos, hair ornaments, and a much lighter color. It became difficult for my sisters and me to fuss with her hair then, although we managed to move clips and pins from one location to another, inevitably releasing tendrils from the strict grip of her lacquer. She grew especially fond of the French twist—the maintenance of which was almost a full-time job. My mother had a cache of objects designed to increase the likelihood she wouldn't have to disassemble the foundation which held the fortress of hair before her shampoo and set a week later. Thus her appearance after emerging from the beauty salon on day one was that of a tight and sophisticated bundle of strawberry blonde hair, until day six when the twist looked more like a sticky bun around her neck.

An extensive wardrobe of hats dictated my mother's hairstyle as well. When she was first married, she resorted to a shorter cut during the summer months, curls framing her face, upswept from her small forehead. Then she would select a hat, usually one with an enormous brim bearing fruit and flowers. Bunches of grapes, purple and shiny, would be arranged between crabapples, plums, and cherries. Floral arrangements were just as complicated. I have pictures of her peeking out from under the fruit and flowers flashing a big smile, looking a bit like Carmen Miranda managing the unwieldy mélange of produce. In the fall and winter, she returned to the French twist and her one black suit with the peplum jacket, a single strand of pearls, and tight hats with discrete veils positioned slightly above the swipe of her manicured brow.

Each week my mother and younger sister, Mary, walked to Hawthorne Beauty Salon which was tucked into a corner of the Hawthorne Shopping Center next to the Hawthorne Barbershop. (Wheaton was the town of spires not inventiveness.) The salon housed one huge stainless-steel dryer, two stations for the stylists, and a waiting area behind a glass front door which, when swung inward, would hit the knees of its patrons. There was a mirror placed at right angles to the door with a glass shelf hinged below which held stuffed dolls with painted pecan heads and cloth bodies. John, my mother's stylist, made them. He painted the pecans either black or a light brown and dressed the dolls in outfits he had sewn. John gave the entire collection to Mary the year that she was recovering from spinal meningitis, polyneuritis, and encephalitis. He carried each doll individually in a tote of sorts, up the hill to our house, and presented them to my sister as encouragement while giving my mother's French twist a little tweak. He did this during the autumn of the year of her recovery, just as the neighborhood was discharging its newest crop of five-year-olds to kindergarten at Hawthorne School. Except for my sister. She had to learn to walk again.

It was their weekly routine, Mary and Mom, both before and after the illnesses, this jaunt of two blocks down the hill from our home on Hawthorne Boulevard and then back with my mother's new coif tied in a chiffon scarf, the ends wound around her neck like a movie star, unless it was raining, and then she used a plastic rain hat. Sometimes they would stop at the Pik 'n Sav for a few groceries and Jell-O Pudding Snacks pilfered by my sister.

I asked my younger sister once if she remembered anything about Mom, prodding her recollection with her travels to the salon, Big Fish Lake, Pik 'n Sav.

"After all," I said, "when we went to the lake, you were stuck in the middle between Patty and me. You had a good view of the whole family for twelve hours!"

"Nothing, really," she replied. "I don't remember a thing about her."

"Nothing? Not even a smell? I mean everyone has an indigenous smell. Perfume or garlic, cloves, body odor, mother's milk? Do you remember Mom smelling like Aqua Net? She couldn't get within five feet of briquettes during the summer."

"Not a thing," Mary said.

I asked her about the nightly drinks, the ubiquitous cocktail hour, the commingling of sweet vermouth, dry vermouth, and Jim Beam. Perfect Manhattans. Cool Tom Collins. The chic Martini.

"No, I don't remember the drinking, then. Just Dad's. After she died."

"But I think you swiped the sweet maraschinos off the kitchen counter. And the mixed nuts. Especially the cashews," I prodded.

"No," Mary said. "Nothing rings a bell."

It seemed Mary didn't have a whisper of recollection about our mother. But then Mary, especially, was robbed of any closure. At least my older sister Patty and I saw our mother last, in death, while Mary saw her last, alive. She never went to the wake or funeral but arrived home after three days with relatives to four place settings instead of five. It was as if we could be denied the horror of mother-death by never speaking of her, pretending she never really existed. Decades later when her brother died, his obituary did not mention Dorothy, the sister who predeceased him.

Maybe all my sister needed was one more glimpse, just one more of her mother, to verify she hadn't been abandoned, not on purpose anyway. That might have been enough to cement into memory the episodes in which she engaged—mother and daughter, the youngest, the baby. I anguished over the loss of her first seven years and tried my best with inept attempts at nurturing, organizing play dates, watching her interaction with other children, encouraging her to talk more, laugh more, be a kid—more.

Mary cared for me as well, slipping into my room gluey homemade books dripping with flower cutouts, crayoned portraits of us facing each other, our brunette heads touching slightly, and carefully copied poems of love. Mother's Day cards accumulated. She continued to do well in school. I started to fail.

Like an archeologist, I struggle to exhume my mother's life, and except for her last day, it remains beyond reach. But *that* day replays itself, over and over and over—vividly. It is inextricably bound to what my life was before the secret, before the end of childhood—not childhood as I was accustomed, no, but *the end of it.* My mother is alive! And I am untainted and steadfast in my belief in fairness. Life is still predictable and lush with her.

The last time my mother dropped me off to ice skate at Northside Park, it was a frigid Saturday morning in January, typical for Illinois. Her hair had been freshly coiffed. It was buoyant, her twist unyielding in the winter chill! My skates were freshly polished with Hollywood Sani-White. I thought them dazzling, but white flakes stippled the upholstery, my coat, gloves, and floor mats. I would find streaks of polish in the car weeks later and frantically scrape at them with my fingernails. My mother was annoyed; my father was fussy about things, especially his Chevies.

"Be careful of the slushpots," she said, swiping at the white flecks that I left behind.

"I'll be home by late afternoon, Mom," I yelled through the closed door. I didn't want her to remind me that I was babysitting that night for my younger sister, Mary, as well as the neighbor's kids. Or that my homework needed to be completed, bedroom tidied, dinner eaten, all in a certain order. My impatience was palpable.

My friends were already on the ice frantically gesturing to hurry up. Without a kiss or a quick hug, I started across the parking lot towards the pond. I don't remember turning to wave either, although that would have been unlike me. I had a superstitious streak. Not to wave would have provoked my general angst. But I don't remember. I often wonder if my mother sat for a minute waiting for me to turn towards her.

A narrow wooden walkway led from the door of the warming hut to a set of icy steps sliced by hundreds of steel blades into an intricate herringbone pattern. The frozen lip of the pond overlapped the very last step, inviting a seamless entry to the initiated. Later in the winter, skaters would have to walk through a few feet of slush to reach the ice, but on this day everything was frozen to a fragile brittleness.

My friends and I rarely skated alone but preferred hanging on to each other, playing crack the whip, our long ponytails slapping our faces, or dancing two by two, switching partners as we passed. We were a formidable line of girls, stitched together four or five across, daring anyone to break our rank. We always skated in the main pond, though, never daring to cross under the wooden bridge, the restricted province of the older skaters. They didn't skate alone either.

Sometimes Patty and I would walk to Northside Park together, slogging through the icy streets with our skates slung over a shoulder, hers just so, and mine, never quite right. Once in sight of the bridge, and boys, I was quickly abandoned. She was a merciless flirt, at least I thought so, and I worried when the other girls stared at her with point-blank hatred, whispering and glaring. Patty didn't notice. Or if she did, she really enjoyed the scene, skating with "her guys" as she called them. Sometimes she would see me and wave, flashing her huge toothy smile, flinging her arms around her boyfriends in mock fragility. My friends were amazed at her nerve. "That's just Patty," I would tell them, digging my skate into the ice, hoping she would skate over to us.

She usually had an entourage to buy her candy, keep her hands warm, and walk her home. But Patty wasn't at the pond that day. She was with our mother, maybe trying a new makeup technique, or hairstyle, or shopping, or gossiping. Perhaps she was helping my mother prepare the house for guests, filling bowls with mixed nuts and laying out small napkins to hold Mom's toast points topped with cream cheese and olives. Mom would be bathing, carefully avoiding her newly arranged hair, while Patty chatted by the side of the tub, taking an occasional *puff* of mom's cigarette. Mom had shown her how—to *puff*, that is, along with some of Patty's friends. She wanted them to do it correctly, inhaling and exhaling, holding and ashing. It was a discipline, Mom reminded Patty, a cigarette discipline, which absolutely forbade walking while smoking. I don't remember my mother ever teaching me anything that deliberately, but I do know Patty and my mother had a special bond. They enjoyed each other's company, like girlfriends. Oh, she had friends, my mother did, friends she shared with my father, couple friends, but no confidante, except for one sister, Aunt Shirley, who lived within an hour of us.

Even though my mother was only thirty-seven, I now suspect she envied Patty's youth and lived vicariously through Patty's popularity. But maybe that is a hazard of motherhood. And is it so bad? As long as it doesn't devolve into enmeshment? Or unrealistic expectations?

Perhaps it did.

As I parse this relationship to glean something of my mother, she remains elusive, overshadowed by the bloom of a daughter larger than life itself. And while my mother may have gained a voice through this flamboyant child, her first-born, she never witnessed the alcoholism and anger that inhabited Patty in adulthood. Was that her legacy? My mother's? Or Patty's attempt to obscure the unique losses associated with this parental relationship. Do children, even as adults, ever become habituated to this calamity?

I walked home from the park that afternoon, a few of my friends with me. Having left little time to thaw our feet by the fire in the warming hut, we hobbled along paths to the main road, slapping our hands to get blood moving in our fingertips, managing to eat the last of our frozen Charleston Chews. We made plans for the next day, a Sunday, to meet in the warming hut again, where we would stash our shoes under benches closest to the fire and chocolate bars deep in the snow, before tiptoeing down to the pond's edge. I promised my friends I would be at the park no later than 2:00, after I attended Mass with my family. My mother would probably want to prepare a brunch with something exotic concocted from her *Gourmet* magazine. Something with eggs, most likely, and a dreaded sauce sprinkled with paprika. I hoped not Eggs Goldenrod. My stomach lurched.

"I might be late," I warned my friends after I remembered the mint jelly filling the center of my grapefruit from that morning which took an inordinate amount of time in which to discretely dispose.

And then it happened—as the fire smoldered in the hearth and leftover shoes grew cold under the benches (how *did* those skaters get home?); as the wind kicked up and deep darkness fell; as a swathe of moonlight bathed the pond and fresh ice crystals dotted the snow; as the pond repaired itself from the assault of blades and misplaced chocolate bars grew brittle; as my friends slept and the night slipped away; my mother died.

"It was a cerebral hemorrhage," my father said after her body was retrieved from their bedroom and loaded into an ambulance. I had been quickly ushered out of the hallway by someone (my father? the doctor?), so as not to see her removed from the house on Hawthorne Boulevard in that final way, in a black body bag. But that was exactly what I wanted. To see. To apologize. For not helping her. That night. I watched from my window which faced the street. The attendants struggled.

"Don't drop her," I mouthed into the cold window pane where I had pressed my forehead. It was 1963, one of the coldest winters on record. The street was slick with ice and the vehicle slipped around the corner, almost toppling. (Someone said at that point I ran after the body screaming "Mother!" or something else equally heart-wrenching in its simplicity. This never happened but made for excellent death-gossip in the neighborhood.)

"The doctor said it was all part of her genetics, her personal makeup," my father announced once again, and for the last time.

"It was a cerebral hemorrhage," my grandmother reported to her two other daughters and one son.

My grandfather filled in the last column for my mother in his genealogical records. Death: Cerebral Hemorrhage. Except he misspelled hemorrhage.

Sometime later, I read about this fatality, the hemorrhage, the Cerebral Vascular Accident, CVA. It sounded like an assembly line problem, a misaligned blood vessel. And, most troubling to me, this genetic malformation wasn't necessarily catastrophic; that there were warning signs (something that would plague me later) such as the severe headaches, dizziness, nausea. Not catastrophic, that was, unless an accident of sufficient proportion occurred, like a blow to the head.

Apparently Dr. DeHaan didn't think so. At least that was the report given to us, by way of our father, as an explanation for this ungodly mayhem. Simply put, Dr. DeHaan said something in her brain bled. It was a cerebral hemorrhage. Who would question that?

"Maybe she had high blood pressure. Or weakened blood vessels. Or an infection. She did have migraines, didn't she? And didn't

she have a weight gain, an inexplicable weight gain? What about her reproductive organs? Wasn't her uterus slipping and sliding, threatening to dislodge itself? She was a time bomb. Genetics. The rupture was just waiting to happen. An accident. CVA! Never knew what hit her. Occurred quickly. She didn't suffer. Nothing could have been done. No one could have saved her. The only explanation? She was predisposed."

Were we, my sisters and I? Predisposed?

But I questioned how Doctor DeHaan could have known for certain that she was felled by a CVA. There had been no autopsy! No Y-Cut! No tiptoe through the intestines! (Where are the superlatives to describe this unfortunate lack of adherence to Illinois law?) Unfortunately, I knew this litany (save our souls) that whirled around our home that morning disregarded one possibility. The cerebral hemorrhage could have been caused by an injury or trauma to the brain.

My hypervigilance awoke me that morning, not any noise my parents were making. But here was the tableau — my father dragging my mother up the hallway to their bedroom. My door was open, and I could see he was struggling. She *was* a little heavy then, full-figured it was called. My father had both of his hands looped under each armpit and clasped together beneath her voluminous breasts. Her silk-stocking feet made a sandpapery sound from sliding on the waxed linoleum, a sound that awakened me from a terrifying dream of a funeral, my mother's funeral, which I dismissed immediately. (This prescience would disassemble any forgiveness I attempted for myself.) But of course I dismissed the dream! Would anyone have paid attention to my ramblings at that hour? A dream in which I am walking through quicksand toward a mound heaped upon a funeral pyre?

I shouldn't feel guilty about not rushing into the hallway at that moment to find solace from my nightmare. I shouldn't.

But I do.

Why was her head slumped forward on her chest? Was she unconscious? And that laborious dragging, my father's labored breathing, the French twist dangling from its girdle—why *didn't* I bolt from my bed?

"How could you have embarrassed me like that?" my father said as they crossed the threshold into their carpeted bedroom. And then the door closed, softly. I don't know how he managed that. To close it so quietly when his hands were so full of Mom. And as I was sorting through what was real and unreal, I heard my mother say, "Don't hurt me."

I didn't try the handle on their bedroom door. Or walk in. I didn't inquire as to what was going on, ask a question, or even say, "I want to see my mother. I just had a nightmare. I'm afraid she's going to die. I need to talk to her." Rather, I rapped on their door and said, "Leave her alone," my lip swelling in the aftermath of my plea. One time was all. Just simply, "leave her alone." I said it for all of us. But I knew it wouldn't be enough. It wasn't. Before sunrise she *was* dead.

I waited for my words "leave her alone" to be returned to me, wrapped neatly in some kind of justifiable account. But there was no explanation that morning as my father wept, holding his head in his hands when he told me to get the doctor, or after he went to confession in his master bedroom between the last rites and funeral potatoes. There was nothing said between us, my father and me, about *any* exchange we might have had, solidifying the diagnosis of cerebral hemorrhage by our omission.

Aunt Shirley arrives, my mother's sister, her best friend. Unlike her, my aunt is a strident woman, a bit officious, but efficient, as demonstrated in the clicking of her heels across the tile floor towards the bedroom where she sweeps the sheets into a pile and dumps them into the hot water of the washer. I hesitate for a moment, my foot hovering over a stain. It seems a rusty blotch has appeared in the carpet. Suddenly. It must be a shadow, an illusion, a colorful floater in my eye. Has Aunt Shirley noticed this defect among all the others?

I follow her; a skittish shadow now, newly infected with the secret, waiting for her, my aunt, to notice my corruption.

"Take care of me, Aunt Shirley!" I scream, but it can't rise above the anguish lodged in my throat.

She is distracted, pale and wild-eyed, shaky, more with anger than with grief. She frightens me into silence.

"I heard something last night," I stutter. *I am trembling as if I have just come in from the front yard, coatless. It is below zero; the boulevard windswept with snow. A day for record keeping.*

"What did you hear? What happened here?" Aunt Shirley hurls at me. "Tell me."

She seems short-tempered and impatient, her coffee sloshing into the saucer as she tries to steady herself for something more. And then it occurs to me that Aunt Shirley has information as well and needs some corroboration. Bed sheets don't lie.

But I knew more and resisted the urge to reenter that night with her. Living with the secret seemed better than the alternative, at least at that moment, at least at thirteen. So I stood there fighting not only with the possibility that I could have stopped my mother's demise, but that I might very well begin my father's. In a sense I started to collude with my father, and for that I hated myself.

My mind became a spectator of itself. It raced, attacked by surging adrenaline. Words pulsed repetitively, "Shut-up, shut-up, shut-up, giddy-up, giddy-up." Mind chatter galloped around the circuitous route of my brain while I stared at my aunt soaking away the clues of the night in Clorox.

"Never mind," I said. "I heard nothing."

She looked at me quizzically and then narrowed her eyes as I turned towards the chatter in the living room where my mother was being eulogized by a choir of adjectives. If only Aunt Shirley had insisted; she was usually so persuasive. But she didn't persist that morning, perhaps cowed by the scene at that moment. And that moment passed.

For years I engaged in dissonant thinking — what I wanted the facts of that night to be, rather than what they were. This perversion took stamina. But I had will power, and persisted, for years, intentionally deluding myself. Pretending was the shield behind which the secret and I lived. It was my only means of self-protection, of survival.

Chapter 2
To the Lake

Traveling to Big Fish Lake required a twelve-hour trip, north-westerly from Chicago, across Wisconsin, over the Mississippi River, and through the Twin Cities. It was a journey of prepositional phrases—over, around, and through—linking city after city with three stops for gas and a picnic lunch at the welcome center on the Wisconsin-Minnesota border.

At five-thirty a.m. on the Saturday before every Memorial Day, my two sisters and I would drag ourselves bleary-eyed to the backseat of our Chevrolet. My father scolded us before we even made it to the garage.

"Empty your bladders, girls. We're not stopping until the Wisconsin border." And with that he popped two aspirin, chugged a hot cup of coffee, lit a cigarette, and got behind the wheel to begin our summer, Memorial Day through Labor Day, on Big Fish Lake.

Patty and I immediately struggled with our backseat territory, making our younger sister sit in the middle between two closely spaced buttons in the upholstery. Patty and I traded off the position directly behind our father. It was a treacherous seat. He could reach around and swat the person indiscriminately when any of us got too loud or whiny. Without the slightest swerve, my father managed these maneuvers. He was a man adept at contortions of mind and body. It was a merciless seat, a seat for the nimble. We learned to bob and duck and lay supine on the floor mat, which made my father angrier and more competitive.

Smells of ripening bananas and apples, liverwurst and pickles emanated from a picnic basket that was placed on the floor in the backseat behind our mother. Cigarette smoke lingered around my father's head. We tried to manage our nausea with Dramamine and small brown lunch sacks kept in our laps until we got our sea-legs around lunchtime. We probably *were* annoying, and more so as the trip lingered on and the day heated up. Cars didn't have air-conditioning in the fifties.

We entertained ourselves with surreptitious fighting interspersed with games of Fish and War and Old Maid. Patty won almost every game. I accused her often of cheating. My mother learned to withhold comic books until the very last vestige of the Illinois border receded from view. We fought over Veronica, Jughead, and Archie. Paper dolls eventually littered the floor, and then their appendages, and ripped outfits. Cherry Ames Student Nurse and Nancy Drew books rested under our feet. Auto bingo ended in squabbles. We tired of taunting truck drivers as my father sped past on two-lane roads, stones ricocheting off the car from the shoulder. He did all the driving, my father, and we learned quickly to suck in our breath oh so quietly. Mary slept on the back window ledge. Her crayons melted in the heat and smeared her clothes. Sometimes, blessedly, she was removed to the front seat so Patty and I could stretch our legs, avoiding skin-to-skin contact at all costs.

We also read Burma Shave Jingles.

Of all the drunks
Who drive on Sunday
Some are still alive on Monday
                    Burma Shave

There were seven hundred of them, Patty found out, all with one intention: to slow drivers down on the two-lane highway.

"Fat chance of that happening," she said. "Dad would rather toss one of us by the side of the road to pee than slow down for anything."

What was the rush? Cocktail Hour.

I don't remember what my mother did on these trips, except that she stayed close to her door and wordlessly shot *the look* to Patty and me throughout the five hundred miles of two-lane traffic. They were pleading looks, looks that took the place of a tight arm squeeze, or sharp "stop it," looks that replaced laughter and conversation. I think she worried the whole day, that the behavior of children she disguised so well on Hawthorne Boulevard, would be supremely manifest in the Chevy sedan.

I'm fairly certain I hadn't complained about needing a bathroom before our 1957 yellow Bel Aire hardtop suddenly lurched out of traffic and came to a rest in front of a pharmacy in some small Midwestern town. I was eight that summer. I probably thought my dad had a sudden craving for something, like a package of cigarettes or maybe some spice drops or candy corn. He had a raging sweet tooth. But then he threw his arm across the back of the seat, tilting it forward for my exit.

"You're out!" he screamed like an umpire with his thumb pointing towards the sidewalk.

"Fini! Over! Get out!"

I was speechless. So was my mother—at least I didn't hear her say, "Now, Tom, isn't this a bit of an overcorrection?" I mean he was notorious for punishments that went far beyond the deed. I blamed his Grandfather Dudeck who frequently called him shithead in German. "*Sheissekopf,* Tommy!" he'd scream at my father in some tormented way. My father had acquired his technique. I thought of this much later, of course, after I came across a picture of Grandpa Dudeck. He looked like Sigmund Freud. At that moment though, I found myself staring at the bobbing heads of my family as the car accelerated into traffic.

I sat on the curb carefully avoiding eye contact. I turned around and read the stenciled words in the pharmacy window.

"Cards...Penny Candy...Stamps...Postcards...Books...Drugs."

I stared in the direction of the car. And I stared the other way. I scratched pictures in the dirt with my shoe and massaged my legs

18

and arms to keep the blood flowing. I did all this without thinking, anticipating their return.

"If you are ever lost," my mother told me when I started kindergarten, "stay in one place and ask a police officer to help you. Just wait where you are and I will find you." That's what she said. But I wasn't certain this counted. After all, my parents knew where I was.

I panicked. What if night came? I was petrified of the dark. I thought of my diminutive great-aunt from Toledo. Her name was Wee Wee. My father's Aunt Wee Wee. She was the only adult in my life who patiently checked under my bed for night monsters. She managed to convince me that if my arm flopped over the side of the mattress, I would not be pulled into the nightmare undertow. She slithered around under my box spring. She opened my closet and stuttered "N-N-N-N-othing is in here." She fluffed the drapes, patted down the covers, opened each drawer, moved books aside on shelves, and left the closet light on. She never complained and she never told me that monsters didn't exist. I longed for her.

I started to pray. That's what Sister Ligouri, my second-grade teacher always suggested. To pray for a miracle. And then go to confession. "You most certainly broke one of the commandments," she would lecture. I tried to remember the Act of Contrition. "Oh my God, I am heartily sorry ..." But I couldn't remember what came next. I *knew* the prayer. I had to memorize it perfectly before I made my first Confession. I tried a Hail Mary. And then a few more. Eventually I lost track.

I worried that a police officer would ask me the phone number at Big Fish Lake. Or the address. I had never memorized them. It was always just Big Fish Lake! The Burke cottage. My grandparents. Florine and Ray. Mups and Gramps! But I knew my address on Hawthorne Boulevard. I decided to tell him that. If a police officer came.

Three years before, when I was five, my mother had threatened me with adoption. It was the summer that I fashioned myself as Annie Oakley, sharpshooter, independent, sassy, speaking in clipped sentences that even a preschooler such as I knew were grammatically incorrect. My father was due to arrive at the lake for a long weekend. My mother was four months pregnant. When she joined me in the Biffy, my grandparents' outhouse, she began speaking earnestly, but then she had that characteristic. And she was perspiring, although in her words she would have been glowing, only men perspired. In the final analysis, however, I should have noticed that I was the only one seated in a three-person Biffy. My mother was standing by the latched door, perhaps holding her nose. I can't imagine the smell was pleasant in the early stages of pregnancy. The image has guided me since, especially in the face of power. Always be wary when you are the only person sitting.

"Your father will put you up for adoption if you are not absolutely perfect this weekend. He told me so last night. He's had a rough week. He can't stand any horseplay. You cannot fight with Patty. Don't talk back. Don't whine. Chew with your mouth closed. Don't frown, or sigh, sass, dabble, putter, or piddle. Just don't monkey around. No horseplay. And smile."

Anyway, as if she were being swallowed by quicksand, her voice rose to a pleading tone—high and breathless as she rushed through the usual animal metaphors. I had done this to her. I had made her beg for my good behavior. There were so many things happening at once, and I was at such an odd angle. My concentration was focused for a moment on my shorts slipping around my ankles, and the sudden increase of my stream, "making water," Annie would have said. And as I tried to maintain balance, perched high above the ground on the canary yellow seat, Patty screamed, "You're it!" through the half-moon window.

"Where would I go?" I asked my mother as she grabbed my arm to steady me. "Does he have a family picked out? Do they live here? Or in Chicago? Will it happen right away? Would I have my own room? Would you visit me?"

And while those may not have been precisely my little girl questions, I vividly remember being intrigued by the prospect, and then frightened.

I stared at her back as she exited and wonder now if she were rushing toward a Miltown, or making my reservation, just in case. My imagination conjured up horrific images, though, more frightening than real life. So I was good. I already knew the enemy and had heard too many fairytales that didn't turn out that well. But my mother's ultimatum did lie scarab-like in my gut, waiting to reemerge. It was only later that I suspected how scared she probably was, her fear overwhelming her. And she was right to be scared: it didn't matter how good I finally became, she would have died anyway.

The heat from the curb seared through my thin shorts. Cigarette butts and candy wrappers whirled in sudden downdrafts. I thought of my mother. And adoption. Was this how it worked? Mice chased each other inside my skull. There was such a tight knot in my throat that it kept the noise that was trying to eke its way to the surface down in my stomach. The sound turned to butterflies. I tried to push them away but they kept flying around, making me feel dizzy. Mice and butterflies. I started to feel sick. When the car nosed itself around the corner, everyone was laughing except for Mary. She was too little. I must have been the joke.

I imagined my father saying, "Look at the stupe!" That was one of his standards. He loved shortening up words. Maybe he thought brevity wouldn't sting as much. My father's sport was sarcasm. He had a particular knack for zeroing in on a weakness. It was his entertainment. He called it "joshing," jabbing your psyche like a lightweight. No remark was veiled in irony. In fact, he prided himself on being brutally honest even though he thought most of the world too dull to "catch his drift," as he would say. He often called Patty and me thin-skinned. I believed him too. His withering glare often felt like a burn.

We learned to deflect his criticism away from victims outside of the family. As we matured, our charming self-disparagement made us the perfect candidates for dinner parties when they required someone good at chatting up the crowd. Don't think it wasn't difficult. I rarely ate a full meal, and frequently used something personal as the catalyst to hilarity. I could hear my father's voice belching from myself at those times and left remorseful like a too-talkative drunk. Later I learned that every eleven minutes in most groups, there was unexpected silence. It was normal. True or not, I found that knowledge a relief. I left my conversation starters at home. I sat in the midst of dinner groups, letting the silence jell the Béarnaise. I became defiant in my resolve to let someone else carry the baton.

"Everything okay?" the host would ask. "You're awfully quiet tonight. Not your usual." My invites fell off a bit.

When I climbed back into the car and situated myself behind my mother, I closed my eyes and remembered my second-grade teacher. She had tried to settle the question of my intelligence that very school year.

"No one can read that fast and comprehend," Sister Ligouri said. "Come here with your book and let me ask you some questions. And thus she proceeded with minutiae about *Madeleine*.

"How many girls stood in each line? What was their teacher's name? Where was the school? Go to the globe and find the country. What color were Madeleine's socks and shoes? Her dress? Where were her parents?"

I told Sister I wasn't sure where her parents were. "Maybe they just left her with Miss Clavell so they could enjoy some peace and quiet. Maybe Madeleine disturbed their cocktail hour. Maybe Madeleine ran away herself?"

Sister Ligouri called my parents. I imagined they talked about books for a while. My father had a substantial hard-cover library, alphabetized, and inscribed in blue ink with his initials 'TCD' on the first page, by the dedication, upper right-hand corner, with his Gold Cross Pen, although he never lent his books to anyone. We were alike in that way, our reverence for books. He selected different titles for my Christmas presents: beginning with The Bobbsey Twins, Honey Bunch, and Nancy Drew, and later, Mark Twain, Edgar Allen Poe, the full complement of Shakespeare plays bound in bright blue cloth, Will and Ariel Durant's *History of Civilization*, books of poetry, and famous people. I did the same for him when I got older. My father most likely thought Sister Ligouri was wasting her time. "Of course, Sister," my father would say in his charming tone, "I understand she can read fast. But I wonder, you know, about her inability to smile, which *is* troubling, don't you agree?"

My school life among the barren nuns of Saint Michael's was a pleasure more complicated than schoolwork. It had to do with *them,* and their devotion to *us,* second only to Christ, their spiritual husbands. (No wonder they were more relaxed than my mother!) For eight years, I flourished within this fold of Catholic school children, the ritualized day a soothing narcotic, a respite from the irascibility of my father.

Sister Marya kneels in the sand, her black habit wound tight around her legs. She places her green cat's eye on the edge of the precisely drawn circle and closes one eye, preparing her attack. Her wimple slips a bit rakishly over her eyebrow. With her thumb, she shoots her marble in the direction of mine, missing it by a hair. She leans into the group of second graders and filches the two glassy spheres, plopping them into the marble bag which hangs on the belt of my navy blue jumper. She leans in close and hugs me tight, whispering, "You are the champ!"

But it is our mothers who are supposed to hold us closest, isn't it? Before my own died, I had absolute faith that somehow she wouldn't let any harm come to me, she would keep me safe, even in the shadow of my father's volatility. I learned it might take a moment, letting him have his way, but eventually I would be allowed to return to the family bosom.

I am Annie Oakley. My brown cowgirl boots are a shade too small but never mind. I am racing up and down the boulevard on my two-wheeler. My vest is fake leather with plastic fringe along the bottom. A skirt rides up over my thighs. I am in a gang of boys. We are all seven years old.

My mother calls to me. I must come home to get Mary bathed. I ignore her. It is a warm fall evening. The light is just dimming with the prospect of fireflies. When I come home later, my father is waiting by the front door. He pounces and screams for me to go. I am a disobedient child. I cannot live here. He is pointing somewhere in the distance.

I look both ways and cross the street. I crouch behind garbage cans, avoiding the maggots squirming in their moist environment. My eyes are trained on my father who is trimming his forsythia. My mother rotates in and out of the front door, exchanges a few words with my father. He waves her away.

Finally, with one roar, my name shoots across the boulevard. "Come home!" And like a dog, I return. Humiliated.

I was certain the car would eventually stop at the toe of my sneaker and I would regain my position somewhere in the backseat. In an eight-year-old world, abandonment of any kind is unthinkable. But I did know all was *not* right, the fear and apprehension—the sense of dread that, while I was too young to articulate, disrupted my sense of stability.

My father's unpredictability was so profound that the only way to counteract its effect was to become hypervigilant. I was, too, all eyes and ears for years, until the big test—the night of my mother's death—which I failed (*The knob! Turn it!*) thus succeeding in releasing my mistrust into something palatable—my father's guilt.

I often wonder if my mother was a consistent source of love, or if her allegiance to my father left her conflicted. Stories of women who allow husbands or boyfriends ill-advised access to their children enthrall me. Their words are hollow like their faces. They don't seem to have a choice. They are stuck. Abductees in their own lives. I try to make sense of my own mother's role in these events of discipline which have the odor of rejection and carelessness. I try to understand her silence. I try to remember if she ever came to me afterward, privately, making sure I knew she was there. For me.

Staring into a photo taken at Big Fish Lake, I look for evidence. I see my fat baby body playing in front of the camera. I can't be more than eighteen months old, pointing at the lens with my pudgy finger, shaping my mouth in a perfect "O." My face is framed with tight blonde curls. My knees are dimpled. My bathing suit is carefully tied around the neck in a floppy bow. I am on the dock that juts into the lake under the protected gaze of my mother.

In another, a little older, I sit upon a rocking horse, mother tucked close, both of us smiling. My sundress looks crisp and white in the sun. Somewhere in these photos, I am being imbued with the best things about my mother. This is what I choose to believe.

I take my own photographs now. Close ups. Faces mainly. Candid shots. I think that I don't trust I will retain what is around me. The shutter of my camera click, click, clicks, with abandon. Too many of my memories refuse to surface; even when prodded and poked like this, they don't respond. Maybe I'm trying to find some familiarity among strangers; something that will resonate with my childhood; something that will become instructive about her.

I turn the camera on myself.

Click.

Chapter 3
Big Fish Lake

As soon as the sign with a large faded red arrow pointing to El Rancho Manana appeared, we dared to imagine the nightmare of the lake trip being over. It was an advertisement for a horseback riding ranch close to the cottage, and to us—the landmark. We started breathing deeply again, thrusting our faces out the back windows to smell the manure from the farmers' fields, waiting until the bank of mailboxes appeared at the top of our road. We took turns walking to those sizzling cylindrical bodies each day, along that dusty lane without a sliver of shade. Horseflies would buzz our ears and catch themselves in our frizzled hair to which we responded with a sort of dancing mania, swinging our arms like propellers. My grandfather had erected a sign by the mailboxes with slats housing a wooden placard for each of the cottage owners on our side of the lake beginning at Peanut Hill with the Cook family, then Coop, Donnelly, Burke, Kelly, Sobkoviak, and around two curves to the Schlenner's.

El Rancho was not far from those mailboxes. The exterior was old barn wood, slivered and cracked from years of neglect. It rambled on in one direction from the front door, without the slightest twist or turn in the facade. Windows were scattered along its length, mostly mud-encrusted, while others, although broken, at least offered a view. The roof line was almost completely flat except for the noticeable sag by the chimney. A sign, impossible to decipher, hung over the door dispelling any notion of a fancy equestrian establishment. I think it said, "Howdy," but I could never be sure.

Trails were sickled through thick grasses between robust stands of trees. Mosquitoes were treacherous and, because the nags barely shuffled us along the narrow paths, we were assaulted through the greasy DEET we had rubbed into our legs and arms.

"Giddy up!" we'd scream, reaching back to slap the rears of our mounts. The horses tolerated us—I don't know how. They never changed their gait no matter what we did. We must have been unbearable with our white tennis shoes and incessant chatter yanking the reins for punctuation.

Emerging from the woods forty-five minutes later, ears twitching in eager anticipation of our dismount, the animals suddenly increased their gait heading towards the slow *snap, snap, snap* of playing cards. Gin rummy, or crazy eights, two decks for double solitaire—Mom and Mups and whichever aunt was visiting were working up a good case of tourista while they waited at a picnic table, sipping Cold Spring Beer and chain-smoking menthol cigarettes to keep the mosquitoes at bay. The resident dog waited too, for pretzel remnants and peanut casings, and a quick sniff of a crotch before he was roundly swatted.

"Rot gut," Patty muttered, scratching furiously at the welts rising on her legs while staring down the dog that came to assist with his moist tongue. "Cold Spring Beer should be banned," she spat, as if it were responsible for the humidity and mosquitoes, and horsey smell infesting our pores. (Manana Ranch was a misery, one to which we begged for year after year.) And then we would hang onto the leather straps hooked to the ceiling of our old lake car as it spit gravel all the way back to the cottages, curbing our complaints from ever reaching the front seat.

Cases of Cold Spring Beer were stacked in the kitchen of both cottages. We could purchase alcohol any day of the week, even on Sunday after the 10:00 mass at Saint Peter and Paul Catholic Church in Richmond. Spirits moved my father to attend services on those Sundays when the beer supply threatened depletion before the Sabbath was laid to rest. Of course it was illegal to purchase on the seventh day in Minnesota, yet extremely convenient from The Middle Bar, The Side Bar, Brinky's, Haffley's, or Jerry's Supper Club. Each had access to an alley, where one case of empties was exchanged for two more, plus tip and the sign of the cross. The large cardboard boxes were loaded by burly breasted men into the back seat of the old lake car where they sat underneath our patent leather pumps, the bottles clinking against one another. For some reason I always felt special.

"Be careful of those bottles, now, girls," one of the adults would say. "Keep the flaps on the box down so they stay safe until we get to the lake." Sometimes we carved dirty words in the cardboard with the crucifix attached to our rosaries.

There were many back roads that led to the lake, not on a map, and impossible to describe to those unfamiliar with the countryside. One that wound its way through fields and small swampy waters with a juncture to the lake was defined by a statue of the Blessed Virgin Mary. She was positioned on a granite pedestal under a small wooden canopy covered with ivy, one hand pointing to Big Fish Lake while the other lay over her breast. BVM's shrine at the juncture was flanked by donation boxes, metal, secured with huge padlocks, and later with wreaths commemorating the deaths of drunken teenagers who careened into her granite kneeler with their Ford pick-ups. We would make multiple pilgrimages to the BVM's shrine and follow Mups and Mom as they approached the statue, hands clasped, eyes cast downward, curtsying when they reached her pale bare feet. Some of the wildflowers pilfered from the roadside were placed artfully around the altar where we would recite a Hail Mary before winding our way back to the old lug of a lake car, avoiding poison ivy as much as the knot of newly minted death.

"God's will," my grandmother muttered under her breath, sounding more wary than convinced.

Grandma quite often knew the families of the deceased and would describe their lives in terms of luck, mostly bad. Luck and God's will. Nobody questioned what a will was, and I didn't either, even though it was the most popular reason given by the Catholic Church for any calamity. The nuns at Saint Michael's, especially, tried to quash our curiosity over death and destruction with those two words, yet never sated our interest, at least not mine. God's will sounded ominous and self-defeating. I would soon learn, though, that we were all projectiles navigating the same trajectory, birth to death. God's will or not. It happened. Sometimes with lightning speed. (Tout de suite, maman.)

The road that ran immediately behind our cottages was dirt, graded most of the time, unless you were unlucky enough to travel in the aftermath of a storm which would uncover years of deep ruts. There was a direct corollary between the amount of precipitation and the height of the corn, snap of the bean, fragrance of the hay, and the number of mufflers and exhaust pipes lying in roadside ditches. With more water came a greater harvest, more vehicle detritus and frequent road maintenance from the Stearns County Highway Department. Grandma's brother, Louie, worked for the highway department, and between Memorial Day and Labor Day, he checked our road frequently. Of course I am sure he wanted to see Grandma. Who wouldn't? Her guests were certain to be treated to enormous quantities of food arranged on colorful Fiestaware in complicated geometric combinations. Perfect for Louie. He was hungry and huge and alone, and could study the platters of food without speaking, as if working out a puzzle, a Rubik's cube of edibility.

Uncle Louie would park his maintenance truck close to the garbage pit that was located behind our lake property. Every cottage had a garbage pit, big compost piles that supplied the fishermen with thick, juicy worms all summer. Tin cans were taken to the county dump, and glass, mostly from Cold Spring Beer, was carefully recycled back to the local taverns.

My sisters and I must have already been symptomatic with our budding eating disorders, so fascinated were the three of us by the girth of this man, his appetite, and his seemingly guilt-free association with food. Observing his obvious pleasure was not only instructive, but hypnotic, as we positioned ourselves on either side of the metal stool Grandma had strategically placed at the head of the table. We didn't giggle either at his derriere hanging on three sides like an awning, although "fanny" jokes were de rigueur in our world. Uncle Louie illustrated a reverence for food so explicit, it was impossible not to notice his slitted eyes, his pulsing temples, glistening forehead and labored breathing as the food made its first appearance. Thickly sliced liverwurst, headcheese, and dark German bread were separated by pungent red onion. There were spreads of mayonnaise and mustard, brown and grainy. Pickled herring floated in sour cream, bacon chunks in the sauerkraut, and warm tangy German potato salad was spiked with an extra bit of special vinegar. Sometimes there were small baked frog legs that looked like they came from stubby chickens, and a tongue, pickled and pore ridden from some unfortunate animal. But the piece de resistance, the dessert, was softened lard flavored with bacon drippings which he sipped from one of Grandma's china cups, saucer included. And then, breaking our trance, Uncle Louie would reach for the jigger filled with toothpicks and use one for each tooth, delicately maneuvering food tidbits off the miniature sabers, until finally he emitted a loud sigh, after which we politely excused ourselves.

In fact, Grandma had a huge family of siblings who lived in the area around Big Fish Lake. Her father had been a deputy sheriff of Stearns County, Minnesota, and she, along with ten other siblings, lived on a coveted plot of land in St. Cloud, a city about twenty-four miles from the lake. The house had been a huge rambling old thing, according to Grandma, with a breezeway that separated the boys' sleeping quarters from the girls'. Trees and wildflowers and an army of squirrels surrounded the main house.

She and my grandfather eventually bought their square cottage on Big Fish Lake, which was near her family homestead, now a Piggly Wiggly Supermarket. We would shop at the Piggly Wiggly once a week during the summer. Mups always parked in the same slot, sometimes waiting a while for a patron to move their vehicle.

"This was the entryway, the beginning of the stone path that would lead you to a dark wood door. The outhouse was here, this was where my father tied his horse, and where my mother sat shelling peas, and this …" Mups would stop and stare. "And this is the place where I had to defeather every damn turkey we ever ate."

No matter the heat in the parking lot, Mups would demonstrate how she ate the turkey neck, the only piece that would be hers.

"I was the youngest female," she said. "And in those days, the boys were fed first, the most, and then more if need be. I'm just glad I never had to eat the Pope's nose."

She would immediately begin to dart her tongue in and out of each imaginary neck cavity, twisting it around bones, poking the tip into minute pockets, and sucking, my lord how she could suck, each and every morsel into her throat. Sometimes she would attract customers making their way into the Piggly Wiggly, customers that Grandma scowled at for parking in one of the bedrooms.

"Can we help you, ma'am?" they would inquire before they saw the tongue popping from her mouth like a viper. I admired her histrionics; how she held our attention in a blistering Piggly Wiggly parking lot was amazing.

(Mups sits on my shoulder like a Magpie. She was so animated. It's no wonder I can recall her stories. And now I wonder if I can attribute to my mother some of the same humor and imagination—a certain *joie de vivre*. Is that cheating?)

In the Land of 10,000 Lakes, Big Fish wasn't the largest (that notoriety went to lower Red Lake, home of the four-pound crappie), nor the smallest. Perhaps Bladder Lake took that honor, or maybe one of the ninety-one Long Lakes, or ninety-one Muds. There were also seventy-six Rice Lakes, three Spunks, one Dirty Nose, an Elbow, a Pug-Hole, and No-ta-she-bun. Fifteen thousand lakes, inhabited by fishermen who believed a little spittle on their bait before casting made the fish bite better dotted Minnesota's landscape. In any direction, at the slightest turn in the horizon, a shimmer of water revealed a familiar stand of fishermen in their tan vests and filthy hats dripping with bait and fish guts.

The periphery of Big Fish Lake was close to six miles if you counted the three coves, two points, bluffs impossible to negotiate, and strands covered with thick, slimy seaweed. The distance across the lake varied from half-mile in some places to three times that distance in front of our cottage. Directly across from us was the public beach where the "townies" went swimming. Sand spread from the lake's edge to the road where cars were parked bumper to bumper on hot days. Patty had a pair of binoculars focused on the public beach throughout most of the summer.

Gramps told me Big Fish Lake was spring fed, which kept it clean and chilly. He called the pockets of freezing water "submarine springs,", which vented into the deepest parts of the lake.

"Be careful, now, Peanut. When you swim into the pool of cold water it goes down *ad infinitum*. Who knows what lives in those pits."

I didn't really know what *ad infinitum* meant but it sounded religious, somehow. I knew the lake gods lived in those cold, deep pits. After all, icons dotted the landscape above ground—watchdogs of our mortal selves—why not water deities? Rock altars dotted the shoreline, most notably housing the Blessed Virgin Mary ensconced in a clamshell. "Mary in the half-shell," my father dubbed them, although many lake residents customized their altars with life vests, fishing lures, and bobbers.

My sisters and I called the frigid areas of water "drop-offs" and straddled them with one leg, treading water in warmth while the other dangled in the cold. I imagined a cone-like structure kept the cold water from seeping into the adjacent areas and secured the lake gods within. I was always cognizant of their presence—aware, somehow that the gods gave the lake its spirit. You could feel it as the current pressed against your body. You could smell it as the season wore on, turning the water from fragrant to thick and sensual, fed by a summer of our stories. Perhaps that was its sustenance more than the underground springs. After my mother died, I was certain I could mine its depth and find our history.

I wrote about the lake that fall after my mother's last visit. I was in eighth grade, a champion word maven, a dictionary always by my side with its plethora of synonyms and antonyms.

"Write about your favorite summer vacation," Miss May Cushing, my teacher, instructed. "Use words from the weekly vocabulary list, and if you can, the advanced list. You'll receive extra credit if you include words of your own choosing, unusual words. Of course, use cursive handwriting and don't forget about the slant of your paper. Pencil only and be cautious about the number of erasures. Keep your paper clean! No holes!" she admonished, strutting between the narrow aisles of our classroom, her matronly hips knocking into our folded arms.

When I look at this piece, I think it remarkable, if for no other reason it survived as evidence of a childhood about to be interrupted. Of what lay in my heart at that moment. If the lake were animate, I would have been accused of being smitten. And I was. It was my first love, right after my mother.

My Summer Vacation by M. Donnelly   *J.M.J.**

Sitting on the edge of Big Fish Lake I can trace its periphery with my eyes shut.

I am a shorebird. If I push the borders just a little they begin to blur as if a sheer curtain is being drawn. I plunge my mind into the Lake's deepest drop-off and lose my breath. I lie on my back to test my peripheral vision and see the tip of Peanut Hill. If I turn a little and curl on my side, I can dip one arm and one leg into the water. I imagine the lake as my womb.

We are both evanescent, the lake and I. We have a consonance of the spirit, an unflappable devotion. My hand runs along its skin and feels nurtured. I plunge into its belly and am protected. I look across its girth and notice the nuance of its gesture. It keeps me buoyant. I line its depths with trust stacked like stone upon stone. It is not unlike a girder upon which I can escape.

Grade VG (Instead of 'E' because of the word "womb.")
*Jesus, Mary, Joseph

On our side of the lake there were two family cottages. My grandparent's cottage was perched high on an embankment which overlooked about half of Big Fish Lake. Its foundation was nothing more than flaking concrete blocks stacked haphazardly between the floorboards and the hard dirt. Although it was damp enough under there to grow mushrooms, the blocks were covered with a white mold that felt like talcum, so dry it leeched into the cracks of your fingers. A lattice skirt encircled the perimeter of the cottage, one section of which was hinged like a gate to allow frequent checks on the progression of the dry rot. My grandfather always did the examination at the beginning of each summer, requiring one of us to crawl behind him holding a flashlight until the saggy floorboards were bolstered with another sculpture of stacked rock.

"Hey, kids," he would say to a group of us, sometimes as many as fourteen planning some game. "Which one of you wants to earn a little money to spend in Richmond this afternoon?"

And then not waiting for an answer, he would embrace one of us in a headlock, knuckling the unlucky scalp back and forth until friction heated the hair. It was never a compliment, being selected by Gramps, to slither through thick cobwebs crawling with spiders, the flashlight shaking in our hand. But we never turned him down. A summer was a long time to be on his bad side.

My grandparents probably owned close to an acre of lake property surrounded by a fussy log fence composed of hundreds of branches of similar size and shape, nailed together in an intricate pattern.

Enclosed within its border was their cottage, white clapboard with an evergreen roof that blended into the branches of trees which were coated with a yellowish gray mold. The branches provided a direct route for the chipmunks and squirrels to hide their stash under the shingles, and to squeeze inside, running along the exposed ceiling joists when the weather turned chilly. It was expected that animals would take over the cottage after we left on Labor Day weekend and would vacate the following May for our return. No traps or poison were ever used. It was just one of the rhythms of the lake.

Architecturally, the cottage was one big square which had a wraparound porch on two sides—until my grandfather enclosed it with huge screens and storm windows, the latter of which could be pulled straight to the ceiling and fastened with metal hooks. The windows would remain hinged to the ceiling for most of the summer, even in the rain, unless the wind blew particularly hard. If a storm swept across the lake when Gramps was away on business, Grandma would throw towels along the edge of the porch and move furniture rather than trying to manipulate the huge sheets of glass.

The porch slanted towards the middle of the house at such a serious angle that toddler cousins would topple and babies would roll on some parts of the floor. Once you got your lake legs, though, splaying your toes and gripping the floor usually sufficed, unless you were tipsy. The porch was filled with wicker chairs and tables, a mish-mash of styles and designs gathered from garage sales and auctions. There were lamps with cloth shades that could accommodate fishing lures stuck into the fabric, some with the remnants of the catch still attached. Rag rugs were strewn every few feet to hide the holes in the linoleum. A picnic table about seven feet long with two matching benches stretched along one whole wall. The table was covered with a slippery green plaid oilcloth that never felt completely dry.

Every lake activity either originated or concluded at the picnic table. Burn holes circled the periphery where small tin ashtrays overflowed with lipstick rimmed menthols and unfiltered Camels.

At night, poker was waged until Bloody Marys were served in the morning, making way for Monopoly tournaments. A Lazy Susan twirled in the middle with the summer staples—Tabasco, capers, a bottle of bitters, a few diaper pins, calamine lotion for poison ivy and poison oak, scissors for haircuts, nail polish, emery boards, a tube of blaze lipstick, matchbooks, and a small bowl of throat lozenges. Grandma read her tea leaves there. Babies were bathed in white enamel tubs, powdered, diapered, and cleared away before the noon meal. Laundry, stiff from hanging in the summer air, was folded and stacked into big piles for each family. A deep fat fryer sat on one end waiting for the Friday night fish fry. Tiny sunfish with gills the color of a rainbow were scaled, rolled in seasoned flour, and dropped into bubbling grease. We ate them like potato chips dipped in tartar sauce.

Within view of the picnic table were two twin beds stashed at the end of the porch behind a bamboo curtain. The beds were for overflow guests, usually adults who had come for the cocktail hour the evening before. People who lived around the lake partied hard. Loud conversations could be heard all night from pontoon boats that idled on the water. Flashlights provided the only light as boaters narrowly avoided collisions with one another. Sometimes when the moon was at its fullest, water skiers would follow its path across the lake. Surprisingly, there were not that many serious accidents, just one spinal cord injury when a boater drove his vessel through a dock with a skier on the back. And of course there was the family who drowned in their sedan, but I didn't consider that an accident.

You might imagine that the cottage was charming after seeing the porch, but in fact it was dank and ill-lit in the interior. A kitchen, two bedrooms, and a large broom closet surrounded a living room just large enough to accommodate a freestanding furnace, a tall wooden table that held an RCA Victrola with LPs on the shelf below, and three old rockers with overstuffed pillows. There were two metal pole lamps with beaded shades plugged into the only outlets. Dusty smelling books and stacks of *National Geographic* were stashed on the shelves that lined the walls, along with photo albums and souvenirs. Cracked and warped linoleum in huge sheets of speckled brown and gray were covered with a circular braided rug.

One summer, before we bought the cottage next door, my grandfather built a bunkroom in the broom closet. He stacked three extra-long, narrow beds on top of each other. They reminded me of vaults in a morgue. He got the mattresses from the damaged surplus store that Burlington Northern operated in Omaha— soft, lumpy mattresses with navy blue striped covers. Before they were even worn in, we would sink in the middle like peas in a shell.

The coveted top bunk was reserved on a rotating basis for the older cousins.

"I don't want any of you falling from the ladder because you had to hurry to use the Biffy in the middle of the night," Grandma would warn.

Of course there was always a porcelain chamber pot underneath the bottom bunk in case of a severe weather event making access to the Biffy difficult. Gramps called it a thunderpot.

It took the skill of an Olympian to clear the railing circling the top bunk, one leg swinging like a pendulum inevitably pocked with bruises from slight miscalculations. Yet even with the wounds and sheer terror of the twelve-foot ladder, that bunk was childhood nirvana. The three-quarter walls provided a birds-eye view of an adjacent guest room where we spied on adults, some whose public and private personas were so disparate it seemed they were Jekyll and Hyde, while others remained consistently irascible, even in slumber.

Summer after summer we rotated through the top bunk, keeping an eye on the room's occupants for anything that resembled sex. Madeleine, or *MG*, as she preferred to be called, slept there when she visited. MG was firmly ensconced in the family after her daughter married my mother's only brother and her son married one of my mother's sisters. Her chain of unfiltered cigarettes gave her a cough so viscous, it was advisable to duck in case something became dislodged. Her skin was dark from the stain of nicotine, and the only time it took on color was when she spoke of her deceased husband. The whites of her eyes were almost completely yellow, her fingernails appeared singed, and long nose hairs conveniently trapped stray tobacco. Madeleine resembled a large piece of peridot.

She had wiry gray hair, huge pores scrubbed free of all make-up, and enormous breasts that melted into her lower abdomen. Madeleine could barely breathe and did so through bared teeth. Her legs were purple from varicosities which leaked through swollen ankles to callused feet as flat as a prairie. She ate doughnuts for hors d'oeuvres, drank straight scotch with a twist, and muttered unintelligibly under her breath. Madeleine's only concession to vanity was a pair of pastel slippers, incongruous under her arthritic weightiness.

No one messed with Madeleine, especially when ordered to give her a peck before bed.

"Goodnight, MG," I whispered, holding my lips frozen, a solid fortress against her five o'clock shadow.

She hissed and squeaked and snored, moving a mountain of phlegm around. You could count on waking at least once each night to the aroma of her Pall Mall stuck between reddened gums as her teeth looked on from a glass of bicarbonate. It was entertainment to which the two other bunkmates might be invited up top. We marveled at the whirligig of these adult behaviors! Sometimes Madeleine threw her matchbooks at us or threatened to climb the ladder herself. The latter threat, while impossible due to her girth, was unsettling to some of the youngest cousins who saw themselves stranded bedside as dreams of Madeleine pulling herself rung by rung, scraping all manner of appendages across the bedsheets filled their sleep.

There was also direct access to the kitchen from the top bunk, via the Hoosier, a portable cabinet whose height coincided with the very top of the partition. Grandma always stacked a box of candy bars up there, a box so large that a full-length fur could have been wrapped in it. She bought the candy from her cousin Coley who ran a café in Richmond—Weibur's Café. Besides the candy bars, Coley sold the best selection of penny candy in the area—wax lips, candy cigarettes in flip top boxes, bubble gum cigars, licorice pipes, Kits, Snaps, BB Bats, Bonomo's Turkish Taffy, edible lipsticks in plastic tubes, and non-pareils in glass containers shaped like animals. She kept them under a grimy glass counter in perfect rows along with tins of snuff and Teaberry Gum. Once each summer, Cousin Coley would come to the lake for dinner. She always wore a white satin half-slip decorated with an intricate pattern of embroidered summer flowers in colorful cross-stitching and French Knots. She wore her slip as a skirt, topping the ensemble off with a white cotton blouse.

Coley and Gramps chattered on about unusual stitches, textured yarn appliqués, and antique taffeta suffused with lamé of gold and silver. Gramps sewed as well, pleating lampshades and adorning them with soutache and braiding that he called French gimp. We had some of his shades scattered around the cottage, along with his hand painted porcelain figurines of women. They were Gibson Girls. He had them cast in full dresses with petticoats, bonnets, and pursed lips painted a vibrant red which clashed with the muted tones of the rose-colored dresses.

Gramps was a man of contradictions rather than a Renaissance man. He was a man of misogynist attributes. For certain, though, he was a welcome relief from Cousin Coley's mother with whom she lived in an apartment in the back of the café. Her mother wore heavy brown army boots with nylons that bagged over her laces, house-dresses in varying shades of gray, and an apron with something faded stamped on it. I always thought it said, "Hook'em and Cook 'em," but I was always afraid to stare too long at the old woman's chest. She was the chef and purchasing agent for all of the candy, the latter to which she applied impeccable taste. At the beginning of each summer, Grandma had the candy bars placed in a box that was printed with Weibur's Café on the lid. Cousin Coley always tied a bright red grosgrain ribbon around it and presented it as a gift, although Grandma paid top dollar for everything she purchased from the café. At least I remember her saying there were no bargains at Weibur's. The box probably held around fifty assorted large bars.

They were distributed at random during the summer but were always in the bottom of the wicker picnic basket when we went to Peanut Hill.

Once a week, my mother and grandmother, giddy with anticipation of a few hours of quiet, would send us off to Peanut Hill with a packed picnic basket. Gramps would have gone back to Omaha and my father, Chicago. It would be weeks before a male would inhabit our female enclave.

(Did *everyone* sigh with relief, become light with less anxiety, take a deep breath, *finally*, and notice that the air tasted delicious? I don't remember ever missing my father as I marinated in my childhood for weeks on end, accumulating memories. Did my mother? Did she willingly give me space to breathe and grow by the sparkling shore? Or was she preoccupied with her own respite? Is it unusual to have a memory so non-committal, so porous, that even as I stretch it like an amoeba to accommodate whatever crumb might fall from these other stories about *her*, its shape remains uninhabited?)

From the distance Peanut Hill appeared to be an appealing parcel of land, shaped like a peanut shell, dotted with trees, and cows, and wildflowers. But rather it was appalling. Once inside the barbed wire fence, the grasses were loaded with mosquitoes, horseflies, spiders, and cow dung. We would spread my mother's blue checkered tablecloth right on the tip of Peanut Hill overlooking the lake, and the sandbars, and within eye shot of our cottages. From there we would spot Mom and Mups lounging in beach chairs on the shore in front of our cottage while we squirmed around the lumps that lay under our cloth. Sometimes we took binoculars, focusing on their animated conversation and laughter, increasing our irritation immeasurably.

"Great!" Patty would say, while nibbling on her peanut butter and jelly sandwich cut into a precise triangle. "We are eating on a pile of cow poop when we aren't even supposed to use public restrooms." Both our parents *were* sticklers about hygiene, restrooms, cleanliness, and germs, but there we were sitting on excrement, eating lunch, in the era of polio. I ignored the palpable disappointment in the adult faces when we returned too soon, while Patty launched into every detail she knew about life in an iron lung. She was dramatic and convincing, ending with a snippet of a poem.

"And now I see you with eye serene

The very pulse of the machine;

A being breathing thoughtful breath,

A traveler between life and death."

"Where did you find that?" I whispered to her after garnering one more candy bar of choice from Grandma's big box.

"William Wordsworth," she said. "It was a love poem. I had to memorize it for Sister Marie Eugenie when she caught me in the boys' wing at school. It was called 'She Was a Phantom of Delight.'"

Patty may have done her homework, but it was clear, the spirit of adult convictions on hot afternoons during the waning days of summer were a little short on action. Polio took a back seat to heat prostration. Towards the end of the summer, we never made it to Peanut Hill but rather ate at various places along the dusty road, taking turns carrying the basket. Sometimes we backtracked to Mrs. Sobkoviak's cottage located a few doors down from Mups. If we were very lucky, she would have just baked ginger cookies, sprinkled with sugar and adorned with half a walnut which she doled out generously. Other times we hid in the barn on our property and never left at all.

Besides the three-layered bunks, my grandfather manically filled his acre of lake property with all manner of ill-constructed outbuildings. I think he might have been creating his own story, a legacy, proof of his own existence beyond his querulousness.

"Peanut," he would say to me. "Say, Peanut, get me that two-by-four and some of those long flat-headed nails." And I would, feeling special and indispensable and needed. Like an assistant to a surgeon or a magician! It was alluring, all his attention, even if we never had a conversation. Even though he filled me with a bit of trepidation. I mean, I would never tell him, "No, Gramps. Can't help you today." There was something about him that made it perilous to turn him down. Anyway, I was dedicated to my grandfather, crawling behind him under buildings like a soldier in combat, my knees wounded with small stones embedded in their flesh.

(Picture this. My mother stands close by, wary, but out of sight. Her hearing is attuned to anything untoward. She doesn't trust this man, her father. He has a temper at the very least. She remains a sentinel until I am released from his service. She physically touches my arm as I run past. Did you see her? Me neither. But still, I create these small episodes that float somewhere in the ether where I stare until my eyes become cloudy with fatigue, signaling a failure of my memory, again. There are details about her and me, mother and second daughter, in all of this. I just need to look harder.)

"We're going to build ourselves a guesthouse, a bunkhouse, a corn crib, an addition to the outhouse, maybe an indoor bathroom," my grandfather would instruct. And suddenly buildings would appear, each made of the same white clapboard as the cottage, this one leaning a bit to the south, or north, that one with a rag tucked between the door jam and frame, a window off center, electricity shorting out. "Peanut, get me a beer, will you, while I straighten up this roof line?" Then he would drink the beer in one swig, belch a great amount of air, and aim his hammer.

There were stone paths leading from the main cottage to every out building and special area that Gramps constructed. And family members and guests adhered to a certain etiquette, an unwritten code of conduct born of necessity, when visiting these structures. Main cottage to corn crib—stop at the squat henhouse, fall to your knees, curse your poor luck, crawl to the cots. Main cottage to guesthouse—single file, sideways, choose bed, notify guest mate to enter, north bed controls light switch. Main cottage to bunkroom—three tiers, more narrow bunks, boys only. Bring comic books and ignore the smell. Main cottage to fish cleaning station—between corn crib and outhouse, wear mosquito netting, bring shovels to bury fish carcasses, spoons to descale, knives to fillet. Main cottage to garbage pit—by road, ripe smell, loaded with earth worms. Walk fast, hold breath, avoid hyperventilation. Main cottage to the shrine of the BVM—genuflect rapidly, spray insect bomb, remove dead flowers, sweep cobwebs, apologize for haste, confess, pray. Main cottage to outhouse (confessional and woodshed)—knock twice, check toilet paper, latch door, be quick.

There was only one building that my grandfather named. He called the outhouse "Biffy." He provided the interior with three seats and a seasonal coat of bright yellow paint. There was electricity for reading, a magazine rack on the wall, and artwork depicting enormous walleyes and northern pikes. The exterior walls had the traditional cutouts, a half-moon and a few stars covered with screens to match. Cobwebs sprouted nightly and were swept away in the morning. Deodorizers were refurbished weekly and rodents removed from traps as needed. But even with all his care, the Biffy was a difficult place in which to relax. There were the flies, of course, which always surprised us when they lit on our exposed backsides, as well as mosquitoes, spiders, moths, and the occasional frog. But, more than all that, the Biffy became the place for parental lectures.

"Finish up, now!" one or the other adult would hiss, followed by, "Be good!" Always the same admonishment, most often unremarkable, no visible tears upon exit, maybe just some residual constipation.

There were thirty-three wooden steps to the shoreline from my grandparents' home, and eventually twenty-six from ours. Each cottage had a long dock jutting into the water from the last step, and a boardwalk that spanned the distance between the two properties where bank met lake. Tall weeds grew down this bank to the boardwalk and were cleared each spring with a sickle. A splintered platform suspended on four empty oil barrels was anchored in deep water for diving and to protect the adults stationed on shore from getting splashed. We called it "the raft."

The lake deposited rocks on our shoreline each night, piles of small stones, colored peach, light rose, or celadon. There were dense pieces of granite that were most beautiful when wet, and others transparent, like rock candy, irregular and smooth all at once. We saved the rocks, tried to identify them, put them on shelves, lined the sides of the steps to the shore, searched among them for arrow heads and shapes of flowers, familiar faces and animals. We skipped them, made fire rings, took our favorites home, and returned each summer to leftover buckets of hundreds more, only to discard them back into the lake.

When he was at the lake, my grandfather continued to rake these rocks each morning before coffee, and evening after cocktails, trying to keep up with the lake bottom repository, attempting to create a sandy beach where none ever existed. (Rake, throw, rake, throw, rake, rake. Grimace.) He coveted the beach connected to our property. A slight turn in the shoreline formed a cove where the water sat glassy and clear, where the minnows swam into your hand if you were still enough. We were separated from that cove by two trees felled by a storm; two huge willows which lay rotting in the water where their tangled branches caught dead fish and seaweed. It was possible to climb over their trunks if you were willing to wade into the water past some old stone steps and some wild blackberry branches that were protected by poison ivy. And it was worth it just to see the smooth, hot sand undulating around a point that literally stretched into the water, forming a sandbar into the shallowest part of the lake bottom, a place where unsuspecting boaters were often beached. The cove was quiet except for the quicksilver *plish* of Walleye that in their exuberance tempted fishermen to their playing fields, fields where I came to believe lake gods dwelled.

There was a certain coexistence of opposites along the shoreline, rock to sand, hills sloping to plains, dense pockets of trees giving sway to sweeps of desert light. The topography of the lake bottom could be deep and rocky and then unexpectedly give rise to thick mud and seaweed. The water was so warm in the summer that it was hard to imagine the depth to which it could freeze in the winter. Fishermen would erect a winter village on its surface, small tin huts with individual stoves grouped so close together that ice skaters could enclose them in figure eights. It was a picture of contentment and simple pleasures, marred only by a submerged sedan.

The story always began with the color of the car. Sky-blue, I was told, solemnly, by my Great Aunt Olivia. "Its color matched the sky on that day, so sad," she said, retrieving her Kleenex from the sleeve of her sweater. We relied on Great-aunt Olivia for the lake news. She and her husband, Jake, lived in Richmond, close enough to the lake to be privy to gossip. Somehow this story of the sky-blue family sedan gripped my imagination. I pictured the children dressed in snowsuits, hats with ear flaps, scarves wound around their necks, mittens clipped to sleeves, and boots lined in fleece matted with cat hair and foot sweat. They were probably laughing (I hoped so), the mother in the front seat saying, "Oh Stan, honey, don't drive so close to the fishing huts," while blowing air kisses from her red lips to startled anglers poking their besotted heads from doorways. Later the fishermen would tell their own stories of Lou and Stan after which they would be hugged by their wives even before their showers. Of course, the wives would never admit it, but the trage-dy offered a respite from the tediousness of fish tales. All the sto-ries would begin the same way: They were taking a shortcut home across the ice.

The fishermen were quick to mark what they believed to be the spot as one of the prime holes for walleye and great northern. I al-ways imagined they believed the bodies provided sustenance and the car some shelter for the prize-winning fish that inhabited that area. They were practitioners, after all, of the art and science of fishing. However, as certain as the fishermen seemed to be that the family sedan had settled in the old fishing hole, I was skeptical. The likelihood that the car plunged straight into one of the deepest lake pits, hood ornament first, was remote. More likely it took its time sashaying back and forth to the rhythm of the AM radio playing, "I Saw Mommy Kissing Santa Claus" or perhaps "O'Tannebaum," riding a cloud of lake foam hundreds of yards from its point of entry into complete darkness.

Patty and I marked the watery gravesite by coordinates on the shoreline and to be safe, extended the area by a few more feet. We rowed around the edges peering into the water with facemasks, imagining bubbles ascending to the surface. With binoculars, we sometimes observed the fishermen, our eyes trained on what they pulled from the water. We felt lucky that we had a smarter father than Stan, and that he loved his Chevy more than anything.

Fortunately for the family in the ill-fated car, that section of the lake was blessed with holy water washed from the bodies of the Benedictine nuns. They had one of the most coveted pieces of property along the shoreline. It was situated between Alexander's Point which cast itself into the lake like a wrestler's arm and a thick forested area on the other. The convent stretched across a grassy lawn, where I guessed the nuns played croquet under the gaze of the Blessed Virgin Mary ensconced in her stone shrine somewhere between the forest, the green grass, and the sandy beach.

We caught them a number of times splashing in the water, their white bodies covered in black bathing suits with straps and boy cut legs. They didn't look that much different from what our mother wore in 1962, except her suits were boned, trussed and reinforced, eliminating any need for straps. Not much older than us, they sported the same blistery acne and late adolescent pudginess that we just assumed vanished upon acceptance of the religious life.

I couldn't completely enjoy the ogling on those afternoons, though. I wondered if we were sinning, all that trolling back and forth in our boat, throwing out fishing lines right in front of the BVM, talking about sex. And if we were, what category? Mortal or venial? Hell or purgatory? Like the nuns, black and white. I asked Patty.

"What's the big deal?" she said with irritation. "We're fishing. Is there a law, or something?"

I wasn't reassured. We had no bait.

"Anyway, what good is it?" Patty sniffed. "You give your life to Christ. For what? An eternal curfew?"

And then she would smile and wave back to the nuns who were swaying in syncopation, their hands keeping perfect rhythm.

"Maybe they want out," Patty yelled as she cranked up the motor. "Let's go ashore!"

She was kidding, of course. She was just simply unable to comprehend the nuns' ability to give up sex for their entire lives.

"Brainwashed! They probably think sex is only for people who can't conceive the Son of God."

We were precocious, Patty and I, about boys and sex and religion. Patty was especially intrigued after having been given "the talk" by my parents one evening during cocktail hour. She had been invited to join them on Hawthorne Boulevard, and as they sipped their Manhattans between illusive descriptions, Patty sank deeper into the overstuffed divan, twisting loose threads from the antimacassar until my father gasped "Stop!" She was scarce on the details when pressed, telling me only that it was much like an amusement ride. But even I noticed we had crossed the slippery slope of venial to mortal that afternoon in front of the Benedictines. I worried. But there was no turning back, especially when Patty was determined.

She was focused on the BVM, who remained a virgin even unto delivery. It was a mystery, we had been told at Saint Michael's School. But then the Blessed Virgin's cousin, Elizabeth, did the same thing, birthing Saint John the Baptist. While divine conception smacked of some genetic abnormality—a mysterious genetic abnormality—Patty had a point. If the holiest individuals were conceived without any sort of foreplay (were apparitions titillating?), maybe the nuns were holding out for their own Savior of the World. If the BVM didn't partake, neither would they.

As luck would have it, in the same area of the lake as the convent, was the worst property—a dark and dank cove riddled with a permanent oil slick from El-Dick's Bait Shop. Only during the most violent storms would the water undulate around El-Dick's. Seaweed remained thick with an odor of gas, and slick fish scales coated the feet of the Blessed Virgin Mary as she peered with some disdain from her perch at the end of Dick's dock.

El-Dick's was a two-story boathouse constructed of crumbling concrete blocks that sat in an eddy of filthy water. I think the owners lived upstairs in an apartment that appeared to be one large room with a huge picture window. In my mind's eye, I see a neon sign in that window blinking, "Bobbers, Beer, Bait". They also sold fishing licenses, rented winter icehouses, and could connect you with the local taxidermist.

Downstairs, a gas pump for boat fuel stood to the right of the double garage door. Trays of night crawlers and angle worms were stacked on top of each other and sometimes placed upon the deep-freeze which held orange sherbet Push-ups, ice cream sandwiches, and Eskimo Pies. Three minnow tanks ran down the center of the shop with shiners, fatheads, and chubs, dripping water, keeping cases of beer, stacked beneath the tanks cold. There were displays of bobbers and loon calls. Bait buckets were stacked five deep and there were always enough locals to make you feel like an interloper.

You never bought a dead minnow at El-Dicks. Someone was always checking the tanks, scooping the floaters with a little net and tossing them out the front of the shop. The path from the shore to the shop was paved with dead minnows. The air rippled with the smell of decay.

When my father purchased the cottage next door to my grandparents in 1960, I remember him tossing the key to my mother with feigned nonchalance. "Here Dorothy," he said, "you have your own kitchen, now!" They smiled at each other across our three heads, the perfect smile of two people in synch—if only for a brief moment. (This memory in its singularity remains divine!) And thus began another path from the main cottage to our house.

It was situated on the same high embankment with one side straddling a gully that separated us from each other. Split-log siding attached to the frame of the house was painted a dark brown and draped with spider webs bulky with millers. The roof was shingled, a flecked-brown color shaded with moss in the spring. On one side of the lot, close to the back door opening to the kitchen, was a well with a red pump. That was the only source of water for the cottage the first summer after its purchase. Pans, buckets, and pitchers were stacked in huge baskets by the well, ready for drinking. We brushed our teeth outside, spitting at chipmunks and bathed with a bar of soap in the lake. We ate mostly on paper plates that summer and burned them afterward in the garbage pit. Utensils and glasses were rinsed in boiled water. My father transformed the pump into a lamp after indoor plumbing was installed. He kept it painted red. Eventually it ended up lighting our summer porch on Hawthorne Boulevard. My mother hung a basket of geraniums on the handle. Regardless of who turned the lamp on or off, the heavy handle was always given a few brisk pumps as if that was the source of electricity.

An outhouse sat close to the back door too, cloaked with a small stand of trees. Unlike my grandparents' beloved Biffy, this building was dark, rank, possessed but a single hole and remained nameless. Frogs hid in the dampness of its interior and when startled, sprayed our legs with their own excretion. There were hundreds of frogs that lived in the tall grasses around the outhouse, some no bigger than a few inches long. We caught them for bait, a nickel a frog. Walleyed pike couldn't resist them, swallowing them whole. Gramps sometimes pulled an intact frog from the gullet of the fish and used it over and over. He said that as long as it could tread water it remained attractive. Those frogs should have earned more than a nickel, but I never mentioned it.

A huge barn was positioned behind the cottage which Gramps coveted. It was painted brown as well and held all the lake cars and lake equipment: a lawnmower, barbecues, different types of water skis, a croquet set, fishing boats, small 3 HP motors, old rods and reels, tackle boxes with lead weights, red and white bobbers, beautiful flies, lures, pocket knives, hooks, remnants of fishing line, inner tubes, rafts, and life jackets. Gramps was given permission to build two changing rooms in the barn, one for the boys and one for the girls. He screwed sturdy hooks in a perfect line for us to hang our clothes and placed benches underneath. Windows were covered with flimsy cotton drapes. On the cement floors were enormous rag rugs. Mosquitoes would lie in wait. The barn gave us some short-lived legitimacy in the countryside of farmers, and for a while we introduced ourselves as "the family with the barn." Then we stretched a curtain the length of its double doors for talent shows and lost our credibility.

Unlike my Grandparent's cottage next door, our house was hidden from the lake by a dense thicket of trees and bushes on the embankment. There were wide concrete and stone steps to the front door flanked by two huge banisters. They were made of the same material as the steps; both shaped like an "s" lying on its back. Patty and I fit perfectly into the scoliosis of the concrete where we would lie after the mosquitoes vanished with the sun, she talking about her boyfriends and me, the lake gods. A path from the front door could take you to the farthest corner of the property, down to the water and a series of jumbled steps, a rotted dock, and an old buoy waiting for a fishing boat. We never used the old dock, except during the summers when Patty and I smoked or later when we brought boyfriends from home. Instead my father and grandfather collaborated on a series of new docks and boardwalks connecting the two cottages and the families.

The interior of the cottage was filled with the possessions of the previous owner. The sale was negotiated that way from a Mrs. Kunkel. She left scores of mismatched dishes, chipped crockery, jelly jars, pitted flatware, stained sheets, pilled wool blankets, pillows, and mattresses discolored from innumerable drooling and enuretic occupants, along with boxes of books that were mostly water damaged and bug ridden.

(I look for my mother in all of this salvage. The way she may have held a chipped cup or plate to the light, covered splintered wicker with pillows, mended rag rugs with slivers of braided fabric, bleached tea towels and stacks of aprons, scrubbed Mason jars to fill with wild daisies, or polished silver and clouded drinking glasses. Exhuming the relics of this old cottage is troubling. And frustrating.)

One large room was divided into a kitchen, dining room, and porch surrounded by three bedrooms. There was no television or radio. Phone communication consisted of three original wooden phones, one in each cottage as well as the boathouse by the water. They worked as a three-way intercom, each with its own code of long and short rings. Paned windows circled the entire cottage. They were in sets and opened inward like small French doors. Each set had a screen to keep out the flies and mosquitoes and curious vermin. The lake powered the breeze through the windows, modulating the temperature from cool mornings toward warm afternoons and then sending it back across its surface to return in the evening. There were half-panel drapes on each window held taut by brass rods; those in the bedrooms were lined with muslin.

The three bedrooms had huge oak dressers, with at least one drawer missing. Chairs woven with a single black diamond in the seat were propped against the walls because of their uneven legs. We looked at our reflections in mottled mirrors hung on rusted chains and stood barefoot on all sizes of braided rugs faded to shades of brown. We hung our clothes on a rod wedged over the top of a door.

The bedroom designated for Patty and me had two twin beds, one of which was directly under the main electrical box. It was an open fuse box exuding electricity as we slept. During storms, my mother would instruct us to share a bed until the lightning subsided.

"Just in case," she'd say. "Nothing is going to happen. It's just a precaution."

That is, until sparks singed the bedsheets during one virulent attack of the lake gods and the beds were shoved together on the opposite side of the room.

By the second summer, the small room next to Patty's and my bedroom had a commode and sink installed. There was a door that led directly to the outside from this room with a large cement stoop that my father made into an outdoor shower. He installed a circular bar from which a plastic curtain liner hung. A soap dish was hinged to the log siding and a towel rack to the outside of the door. The water for the shower was pumped from the lake, freezing from June through August.

My parents were in the bedroom that faced the lake, three rooms away in a lumpy double bed that groaned along with them when my father arrived for his visits. Mary slept in the middle room with the sole closet in the entire cottage and an extra bed for guests. The only room that had an actual ceiling was the bathroom. All the others were encased in plywood walls jutting three quarters of the way to the exposed roof supports where conversations floated into the night. I cursed my watchfulness on those nights when I heard my father's voice, sleepy and slow as it slid up and over the walls that surrounded his bed.

"Now this is what I missed," he said.

Instinctively I knew to be embarrassed, that this was none of my business, that my father had just admitted he had needs beyond the capability of the Perfect Manhattan. I just knew it had something to do with my mother's breasts, for some reason I could picture him snuggled into the never-ending chasm—her cleavage. My imagination made me nervous. I squeezed my eyeballs shut until my brain could readjust and only a dot of red appeared. And then, my worst nightmare, the word, "breast" began rumbling by in capital letters. "B...R...E...A...S...T"

The letters danced and turned on their heads. They toppled as they tried to make a tower. Individually each letter moved to the front of my skull and then retreated. I settled in for the long haul, wrapping my pillowcase around my head. I twisted excess fabric into spirals and stuffed my ears with the 200-count cotton pillowcase, hummed, counted, and waited for morning.

I did worry about my mother. I wanted my father to love her as much as his Perfect Manhattan. It was that square little cottage with its three-quarter walls that gave me a modicum of relief that night. It might have been the first time I recognized my parents had a private life, a secret language, something other than what I witnessed. Immensely embarrassed the next morning, I tried to sense something different in their relationship, a little more of her, and less of him.

But she remained vague, and I can only surmise that like me, she continued to be cautious, nervous, and submissive, lacking spontaneity unless Mr. Manhattan swept his arm across her shoulders. Only then might she overreach, let down her guard a little, to which my father responded by slamming the front door, leaving hairline cracks in our psyches.

I didn't really understand the coexistence of harmony and disorder the year that Patty and I exuberantly traveled around the lake shore taking apart the truth as we had been taught. The next season, it made sense. We traveled with mother-death then, and wondered how the lake could remain beautiful when our world had collapsed. Patty and I didn't talk much that summer, but we trolled quite a bit. This time, when we stopped in front of the Benedictine Convent, we didn't pretend to cast our bait, preferring instead to stare at the blurry shapes of the nuns, letting the water coagulate in the stifling air. And the smell of El-Dick's? It had become familiar.

Chapter 4
The Boulevard

As soon as he could afford it, my father found a tract of land in Wheaton, a suburb twenty-five miles west of the Loop in Chicago, from where he commuted to Sears Roebuck five days a week in his charcoal gray suit and polished black wingtips. Wheaton, which boasted fifty-two parks, the first eighteen-hole golf course in the United States, and The Popcorn Shop, a store no bigger than a narrow alley filled front to back with penny candy and nickel bags of popcorn, was just one of many beads strung along the railway. Yet, even with all those parks and popcorn, this particular suburb had one huge omission: it was void of liquor stores and bars. Wheaton was dry.

Patty and I were toddlers when he built our little ranch house with a front door that changed colors while the clapboard siding stayed white and the shutters, black. The door was notable, heralding the popular colors through the 1950s— harvest gold, gypsy red, and glacier blue. Once he painted the door the color of our two-tone Chevy, avocado, and trimmed the three diagonal windows in a brighter shade, not quite yellow, but close. The front door was framed with a wrought iron railing that had curlicues for holding evergreen boughs or flowering spring branches, a task my father accomplished deftly as one season blended into the next.

The house was called a "starter home," a description that elicited words like fledgling, beginner, training wheels, temporary. This particular "starter" grew up over seventeen years with a longer hallway, one more bathroom, and master bedroom which my father called a "suite." The utility room became a family room and the back patio was screened in and tiled as a summer living room. The garage was for two cars although we never had more than one. A large workbench was parked in the extra pad and held an enviable assortment of Craftsmen Tools, which became mine after my father died. I never did learn how to use any of them except the level, which was a rugged piece of metal with one cracked viewing window. On the roof of the two-car garage was a cupola with a weathervane shaped like a rooster. During the Christmas holiday, an enormous evergreen wreath hung on its side, facing south, with a red ribbon that invariably became tangled around the rooster's neck. A spotlight nailed to the end of a two by four and mounted on the side of an eave was focused on the wreath for a full month.

Hawthorne Boulevard was designed as three blocks of grass bordered by a canopy of elms. Every family took pride in the boulevard, fertilizing and staking the fledgling elms, paying kids a penny for every dandelion removed by the root, mowing, raking, and trimming the areas of grass and trees which lay directly in front of their homes. At the end of October, each family raked leaves from the boulevard into the street and lit individual bonfires. It was always the dads casting long shadows into the street who tended the fires. Acrid smells still remind me of my father leaning on his rake, sipping his coffee or cocktail, talking to the neighbors, putting a proprietary hand on our shoulders when we got too near the flames. He whittled sharp tips on the ends of sticks for marshmallows and ate them with us if they were charred enough. He poked holes in metal jar lids so that the few remaining fireflies from summer could breathe as we raced around during nightfall, holding our containers like flashlights. I loved my father on those autumn evenings, in his plaid lumberjack shirt and old brown leather boots. I loved the smell of him, of smoke and cigarettes and strong alcohol. He seemed satisfied.

I collected leaves from our American elm, sugar maple, and weeping birch, selected those with the densest color and best symmetry to iron between pieces of wax paper. Year after year, I bound the pages together with yarn and listened to the distinctive rustle of the familiar music, fall music, as I turned each page. *Ulmus americana, Acer sacchaum, Betula pendula*—the strings of my instrument. And then Dutch elm disease wiped out the boulevard.

My bedroom, which faced the wide street, was enveloped by its shadow. In the darkness of the summer nights, it wasn't the sound of cicadas that I heard but the hiss of DDT trucks making their way down the street. I watched through a slight crack in my shutters, and even though my windows were closed, I could smell the odor of chemicals—an odor I had smelled for years, but in 1960, when I was eleven, it occurred to me that it was aberrant. My throat would tickle and I'd cough over and over until at last a spasm ended the siege. My father said it was hypochondria.

The leaves, laden with a thick liquid, oozed stickiness onto sidewalks and toys. DDT became part of our sand and garden soil. When we ran barefoot along the boulevard, the chemicals became part of us. The pungent smell never completely dissipated for weeks but would regenerate in the heat of the following day. The spray was our summer night music emitted from trucks that inched stealthily along the boulevard to save the mighty elms from bark beetles. But they lived—the beetles did, while birds died, people got cancer, and the boulevard became denuded. I abandoned leaf ironing. The autumn burn became unnecessary. My world was threatened with monochromatism.

While my father created a diverse landscape surrounding our property, he clearly preferred a simpler taxonomic structure when it came to human relationships—superior and subordinate. The first lesson I can remember was pansy Jew, a term he used to describe some buyers from New York who worked with him at Sears. It all started with their fingernails, polished with a clear lacquer, and then buffed to a high sheen, showing the whiteness of the tip and smooth nail beds. My father was very particular about his own nails which was why it was confusing, this apparent disgust over hygiene.

I remember I told him pansy meant "thought" in French. "*P-e-n-s-e-e,*" I spelled for him. I think I told him how much Georgia O'Keefe loved them. I was in fifth grade then and had chosen New Mexico as my state to study. (Unaware of the sexual connotations proliferating from the stamen of her flowers and nodes of the seashells, I particularly liked her purple pansies, much to the chagrin of Sister Lavinia. She told me to concentrate on the oil painting called "Black Cross" which hung in the Art Institute of Chicago.) But I could tell he wanted me to be quiet. His mouth had settled into a hyphen by then. I learned to be silent during these diatribes, yet that seemed to signal my complicity. It was a sticky wicket.

This was just the beginning, the first lesson that I can remember. I later learned that the *Pansy jew* was just one subset to the *Homo sapien*. There were many more. *Inferior africanus, italianus, mexicanus, feminus,* all charted after *Homo erectus* and before *Cro-magnon.* Carolus Linnaeus be damned.

I knew he was wrong. Even as a young adolescent. Maybe my mother counteracted his "isms." I don't remember. But my father and I would fight over his selectivity as I matured.

"What do you see wrong in this ad?" he snarls in disgust, throwing the newspaper in front of me. We are sitting at the breakfast table. I am in high school.

It's a test. One which I will flunk. Again. I stare at the picture. It is a Sears advertisement for their portrait studio. I read quickly. It seems all they want to do is "capture the tenderness of an age and the personality of the child."

"I don't know, Dad. I just see a little girl. And a coupon." I stare until my eyes water, wondering what it is that has offended him.

"What! The child is black! Dark black! You don't see that? My god. What is Sears thinking? They'll lose customers over this."

I feel like I should say something. But I don't. I know my place falls somewhere within his inferior class system as well. Does he see me as a receptacle to fill with vitriol? My hatefulness keeps me steady.

(A few years after my mother died, my father began surrounding himself with male companionship rather than female. He never explained a thing to me or my sisters, but as always fortified himself with alcohol and then bluster to keep any inquiry at bay. Was he conflicted about his sexuality? At least that would have been some explanation for his anger.)

While my father's beliefs created contrived barriers, they were natural in our yard—vistas, flowers, trees, and shrubs. Chinese snowball bushes lined the backyard, blending into purple lilacs on one side of the property, and on the other were the forsythia bushes. He fashioned them into works of art, making clean, precise cuts with special pruning shears and painting the wounds with a special mixture to keep insects out. It was a wonder then with all of this tenderness directed at his plantings, that Patty and I were allowed to pursue our circus plan threatening his landscape with our three rings.

Actually the circus was my idea, but I knew I had to convince Patty to participate. Although there was no one else like her, a born performer with goals that never wavered, her free time was scarce, most of it spent currying the favor of boys and searching for reflective objects. My mother called her "boy crazy" and "vain."

She said, "Patty, there isn't a mirror in the world that can show what you really look like."

"That's why I keep trying," Patty said.

Her three goals in life were to be a cheerleader in high school, a majorette in college, and Miss America. She wanted her career path to lead her to the cool waters of Esther Williams. She wanted to continue the legend of Esther, wear bathing suits with high heels and a sash that spelled out *Illinois* across her chest. When she came up for air, she wanted masculine breath to dry her brow. She wanted to be in the center ring. She said, "Yes," when I asked her to be in the backyard circus. "But only after charm school is completed," Patty said. "And that depends on how well I do on the final exam." I wasn't worried. Patty had been practicing for months walking with a book on top of her head and crossing her legs demurely ankle over ankle as directed by her instructors at the Patricia Stevens School of Charm.

Patty wanted the circus to be part cultural, part cunning. She wanted to play the piano piece that she was perfecting for the Miss America contest. She managed to learn only three pieces in as many years of lessons and ingeniously strung them together into a medley equaling twelve minutes of repetitive music. My mother told her we could open a window in front of the piano and seat the guests in a semi-circle on the lawn outside. A peony bush needed trimming, though, and pruning was out of season just then. My father would need to be consulted. And then the ants were discovered feeding on the aphids, feeding on the flowers. The area was sticky with excrement. It could be tracked into the house. "This area is quarantined," my father said. "I will have to spray immediately." My throat closed. The cultural event was canceled.

Patty didn't need her Miss America medley to dominate the circus events after all. It was her control over the baton, her stage presence, and perfectly flipped hair that stole the show. Almost shoulder length, her flip was so tight, one of her acts was to roll a marble from one end of the flip to the other—cheek to cheek, without it ever breaking through the tube of hair. Her flip never budged as she threw her aluminum baton over her head, under her legs, to each side, and into the audience, her pale arms a blur. The baton almost screamed with delight!

She marched along the periphery of the guests, all of them women in shirtwaists and high heels coated with dirt from inadvertently aerating the lawn. Our mother popped popcorn, stirred Kool-aid, and served fresh coffee, weaving in and out of the two rows of chairs. A few of Patty's boyfriends crouched in the back, underneath the bushes, and watched her red and white striped halter ripple with the vigorous pumping of her knees and arms. With her back swayed, looking triumphant, her face catching the full force of the sun, she opened the show.

"She's a grand old flag
She's a high-flying flag,
And forever in peace may she wave.

She's the emblem of,
The land I love.
The home of the free and the brave.

Every heart beats true,
For the red, white and blue.
With never a boast or a brag.

Should old acquaintance be forgot
Keep your eye on the grand old flag."

The hollow baton had so many scratches and dents Patty wrapped it with crepe paper to match her outfit. She used it for balance to walk the tightrope that we had stretched between two trees. She used it to tame our neighbor's beagle. She threw it on the ground and did some kind of jig back and forth, back and forth, a whir of appendages! She balanced it on her knee and palm and shoulder. She placed it lengthwise on the top of her head and walked ramrod straight through the audience. But no matter what she did with the baton, it was how she used it during the commercials for Ipana Toothpaste and Good & Plenty candy that brought the house down. Patty came from behind a bush with her arm swinging the baton like a wheel of a locomotive chanting, *"Good & Plenty, Good & Plenty, Good & Plenty, Plenty Good."* She snaked in and out of the metal chairs with her baton in one hand and pink and white Good & Plenty in the other, dropping a few into the skirts of the moms and the open mouths of her boyfriends. Then, after a brief chug off stage where she ripped the crepe paper from the baton she emerged with it as an imaginary toothbrush, smiling broadly, singing, *"Brush-a, brush-a, brush-a, with the new Ipana ... toothpaste!"* She made brushing motions in front of her teeth with the baton and after tossing it into the air, she twirled on her feet, disappearing into the forsythia.

I suggested at one point that we do a Doublemint commercial, be the Doublemint Twins. We could use the baton, I said, and toss it back and forth while we sing, *"Double your pleasure, double your fun, with Doublemint, Doublemint, Doublemint Gum."* I told her we could wear white blouses and our school uniform skirts with knee-highs. I gave her permission to roll my hair in juice cans so I would have a flip too. "I'll even sleep on the cans," I said, although I knew they left dents in your scalp.

But my flip never equaled hers in structure. I ended up hopping around on my pogo stick during Patty's transition between acts. I bounced around the audience, until she emerged from the bushes. I bounced until I was dizzy. Sometimes I lost control and pogoed out of sight. My father was angry about the indentations in his lawn.

The following summer, the forsythia corner of our yard took on another persona, different in some respects than the circus but very similar. The ten-by-eight-foot rectangle staked with burly hemp rope from the lake was the proposed site of our family bomb shelter. Patty struck back immediately. She had been determined to salvage the cultural part of our circus idea that year with a repetition of a prayer—in song—that was guaranteed to shave some time off purgatory.

"Look," she said. "I have worked on the song *Salve Regina* for two months. Maybe even longer—whenever I finished studying the French Revolution. Anyway, Sister Clemencita told us about an entire convent of Carmelite nuns who walked to their deaths singing the *Salve Regina*. The high notes are killers. *O clemens, O Pia, O dulcis, Maria*! I want to sing the *Salve*!" she insisted. "Sister said it was from an Opera called *Dialogues of the Carmelites*." My part was going to be "The Walk to the Guillotine."

I was relieved my father said, "Absolutely not and no questions." Even to him, a non-believer, I think it sounded sacrilegious. Besides, my father was distracted with Commies and Sputnik, followed by Elvis Presley. The impetus, however, to send for pamphlets on bomb shelters began with the introduction of Tang. "Screwdrivers," my father noted. "Tang, vodka, and water. Not perfect, but passable."

"Do you have any idea what this means?" I hissed to Patty after thumbing through the pamphlet, "You Can Survive," from the Peace-O-Mind Shelter Company. "We might be living in a one-bedroom bomb bungalow. We have to be vigilant."

My father carried a clipboard to the roped site each evening after work. My mother teetered after him in her white pedal pushers and heels with a tray of Manhattans and a small bowl of mixed nuts. There they sat elbow to elbow in a redwood loveseat situated in the middle of the proposed roofline. They imagined how an eighteen-inch-thick outer wall would look. They discussed whether they needed a radiation barrier, a generator, two-way radio; they debated the lifespan of "AA" batteries. My sisters and I were to decide which three things we wanted to bring into the bomb shelter to keep us occupied for a few months. They worried over food, clothing, entertainment, and medication and became disenchanted whenever defecation was mentioned. However, it was the prospect of running out of alcohol before the radiation had completely dissipated that bothered my parents most.

"And ice," I reminded them when I caught their attention as they stirred another batch. "What are you going to do about ice and refrigerating the maraschinos?"

We weren't naive, Patty and I. Lack of access to the Gables Bar and Package Store could be worse than an H-bomb.

They lost interest in the bomb shelter as the summer waned, the weather cooled, and the forsythia lost their leaves. The debate about the morality of shooting neighbors if they tried to break into your shelter had run its course. Living underground in lead-lined pj's became passé. By September, when the redwood furniture was put back into storage, the hemp rope was raked into the street for leaf burning.

The only relative besides Mups who visited us often on Hawthorne Blvd. was diminutive Aunt Wee Wee, until her psoriasis became more pronounced and some skin was found on our kitchen counter. Despite her height (four and a half feet), her monotonous stutter, and obvious favoritism towards me, she wasn't cowed by my father. Standing in her teeny black pumps and starched shirtwaist, Aunt Wee Wee would often bob her cap of tight white curls at my father, saying "N-N-Now Tom! I d-d-don't think that's r-r-right." Sometimes she would take my arm into her hand and hold tight for just a second, or find my eyes across a room and wink. She would collude with me over vegetables, distracting my parents as I cleaned the pile under my chair, having slid enough peas, or carrots, or beets onto the floor to be excused. Aunt Wee Wee mended my favorite clothes, laughed at my jokes, and let me read *Eloise* to her every night. She gave me a picture book of *The Lord's Prayer* and an old cream pitcher with a black Scotty painted on the side. I still have them both.

My most vivid memory of Aunt Wee Wee was during a horrendous snowstorm in February of 1955. We were traveling to Saint Charles Hospital to retrieve our mother who had just given birth to Mary. Aunt Wee Wee and I were huddled together in the backseat of our Bel-Aire Chevrolet Coupe. The Chevy boasted the first ever wraparound windshield, which in this particular case provided more surface area for the rapid accumulation of snow. The defroster wasn't working, or at least not fast enough, and Patty was wiping a perfect circle in the windshield with my father's monogrammed Irish linen hankie. His initials, TCD, were unraveling, leaving trails of thready hairline fractures in the glass. I remember wondering how my father could see at all, even through that perfect little circle, when his hat was pulled so low on his forehead. The fins on the rear of the car wiggled like a shark when we hit ice; Aunt Wee Wee was shedding skin like a snake. She squeezed my shoulder and whispered that I would need to open my eyes eventually, and then went on to assure me I would learn to like Mary. She said something about a second skin and I worried about that image for years.

For some reason her presence made my father kinder, a bit gentler, even though he considered her an interloper when she moved into his childhood home, after my grandmother, Wee Wee's sister, died of complications from a broken hip. She moved in to help with Grandpa's transition to widower and never left. I think the arrangement caused my father some angst. He thought she was freeloading (a mortal sin in his view), that she needed to earn the right to live on Evansdale Avenue in that ancient little cottage which was separated from the sidewalk by a strip of lawn the width of one swipe by a hand mower. You could tell he had a strong sense of ownership and pride in the leaded-glass bookcases, the huge clawfoot tub that required a stepstool to clear the rolled porcelain edge, the enormous elm in the backyard, the turn in the front staircase where his nephew entertained us with plays, and the dark cellar littered with wine-making paraphernalia. He rubbed the silver spoons in the sterling cup that sat on an oak sideboard with his white handkerchief until they shined. He organized the books and magazines cluttering the living room and soaked doilies in Ivory Flakes after they had yellowed while adorning chairs and tables. He beat the braided rugs and put wax on the wood floors. Nothing was ever thrown away that had what he called potential. Cracked, chipped, warped, scratched, discolored, or mottled equaled patina, which equaled a treasure. I always admired his "eye" as he called it.

At the end of every school day, I knew my mother was waiting on the Boulevard. My lunch was prepared in a metal lunch pail with a wide-mouthed thermos that contained hot chicken noodle soup in the winter. Her name was written on the back of each of my report cards until eighth grade. Meals were plentiful. And even though I don't recall any specific birthday or Christmas celebration, I would have if they hadn't been consistently observed. My Brownie and Girl Scout uniforms were impeccably ironed; the badges sewn precisely with a slip stitch. Each Easter my sisters and I had spring coats, straw hats, and new patent leather Mary Jane's. We wore short white gloves and carried little purses that contained a starched handkerchief with an embroidered shamrock. She provided cloth jump ropes with wood handles, roller skate keys knotted to ribbons for my neck, and a suede marble bag heavy with boulders, steelies, and cat's eyes. She sewed an entire wardrobe of clothes for my Madame Alexander doll—hats and coats with tiny buttons, a Brownie uniform to match my own, gowns with petticoats, shorts and tops which buttoned down the back and packed them into a blue trunk. When I was interested in the different shapes of snowflakes, she gave me a microscope for Christmas and didn't laugh when I set my sights on being a pediatrician. Frequently she and I made trips to the old Wheaton Public Library where we would pass the crouching lions flanking the heavy oak door while heading to the second floor, the children's room. There I would stack books in a pile by where she sat, and she would count them until I reached the library limit.

It was most likely my mother's idea that I attend the Kiwanis Club Daddy-Daughter Dance the year I turned eight, an event which filled me with apprehension even though Patty had already taken her turn without any apparent ill-effects. However, I feared being alone with him could turn hazardous, especially without the buffer of my mother, although I had to admit even in her presence I had been left by a few waysides.

No doubt, the date *was* alluring—he was so handsome—his eyes icy blue and hair, thick and wavy. Plus, he could be charming. Supremely so! At least women seemed to enjoy his attention, leaning closer to savor his comments, frequently nodding and touching and staring. Even men hung their arms loosely around his shoulder in some secretive confidence. Why wouldn't I be flattered that I was *his*, this one night, despite the fact that I annoyed him? Clearly his tolerance for me, maybe even his love, emanated from a very small aperture. At least I never felt like I could fill his frame no matter the effort.

I love you, my naive heart sang.

My mother reassured me that my father and I clashed because we were so much alike. Eventually I became horrified with the comparison and changed the slant of my handwriting because it was almost identical to his cursive; rejected his racism; and when

I found out he had chosen my nickname, Mickey, I changed the spelling. I drank straight alcohol when he preferred mixed drinks. I was a Democrat, liked the Kennedys, attended Mass, read nonfiction, loved poetry, the *Chicago Sun Times,* and the Volkswagen Beetle, all of which he despised. But that was a long while after our one and only daddy-daughter date. Back then I unashamedly tried to make him like me.

With an eye toward rapprochement, my mother bought me a new dress and attempted to minimize the scratches on my patent shoes with a heavy coat of Vaseline. Instead of allowing me to wear my ponytail high on my head as I preferred, she pulled my hair back and fastened it low with a ribbon to match the sash on my dress. "That's how your father likes it," she said. My anklets were white, my gloves almost, and in my purse I carried an ironed hankie that my great Aunt Wee Wee had given me for my first communion. I also threw in a pair of rosary beads and a few of my favorite marbles.

"You'll be fine," my mother said. "You'll do fine."

We weren't even through the "tie the tie" contest when he began to wince each time I wrapped and unwrapped the fabric around his neck, crossing the long tail with the short, flipping it under, over and through, until the knot, perfectly squared, was pulled taut to his throat. I should have stopped after I flipped his starched collar up and poked the end into his cheek, but it was the only way I knew to adjust the tie length so the fabric would lie flat. It was one of the activities on the invitation that I had practiced in front of my mirror on an old tie with a pattern of martini olives. My father finally did it himself, disqualifying us from the contest. I scuffed his wingtips when we danced and made one of his pant legs greasy from my shoes. I accidentally wiped my mouth on the front of his white shirt, leaving a small brown smudge from the dessert, and flipped my ponytail with such vigor during the two-step that it slapped his head. I lost my father somewhere between the Hokey Pokey and the Bunny Hop. One of the other fathers told me he was outside having a smoke.

It was my mother who wanted us schooled by the nuns at Saint Michael's and then later Saint Francis High School. She made certain we were baptized, made our first confessions and thereafter whispered our sins to a priest each Saturday. She sewed our white lacy communion dresses and found small veils which we wore as a symbol of our purity. When we turned eleven, we received the sacrament of Confirmation, becoming soldiers of Christ. And each year she helped me buy a pagan baby by donating pennies from the milk jug which sat on a shelf in her sewing room.

Buying pagan babies was a Catholic school program which encouraged students to send their money to poor countries so babies could be baptized Christian. By the time I was thirteen, I owned eight.

I heard about pagan babies from Sister Marya, my first-grade teacher who developed a Valentine's Day theme called something like "Pennies for Pagans." The idea became a school-wide project.

"You can bring in money and adopt a pagan baby," Sister Marya said to our class. I can picture her strolling between our straight rows of desks, the heavy rosary beads which cinched her black woolen habit at the waist slapping against us. We sat perfectly still, clenched hands in plain view, eyes forward, feet on the floor, straight backs. I'm pretty certain Sister Marya smelled like stew that day. Most of the nuns at Saint Michael's had a meaty smell if you got too close.

"You can save those babies," sister Marya continued, "with your pennies and nickels and dimes." (Oh my!) "You can keep them from ever having to spend the rest of their days in limbo. We'll have a contest!"

We all knew about limbo. Sister Marya said it bordered hell. I pictured it as a place where little round souls bobbled into each other aimlessly, never getting anywhere. There was no chance of getting into heaven once you landed in limbo if you were a baby. Heaven was reserved for the baptized, the believers in the one true faith, the chosen ones, the Catholics. No wonder we felt so smug. Sure, some of the baptized would make a stop in purgatory for a few thousand years of personal suffering, but at least heaven was available.

"There are clocks in purgatory, children—just you, some heat, and the ticking clock along with your very worst enemy," the nuns told us. "Remember, though," their voices increasing in volume, "you will *eventually* reach heaven. Imagine going to limbo forever because you were a heathen."

At least limbo didn't have a clock, I thought. Or your worst enemy. What's wrong with neutral? Not too happy, or too sad. Balance. I thought people meditated for that state. But our job was to get the pagan babies baptized, giving them a shot at hell and purgatory.

The rules were simple: design a poster with a religious theme, attach some money, and bring it to school on Valentine's Day. The projects were displayed until they buckled under the weight of pasted pennies. We would spend the morning of the contest with our arms folded behind our backs walking through each classroom, voting on a winner. There was the Blessed Virgin, arms outstretched, pennies descending from her fingertips like water, her head encircled with a halo of dimes; the manger of the Christ Child feathered with a fin; martyred saints pelted with pennies instead of stones; guillotines glinting with silver; clothing fashioned out of bills. Some of the posters required 3-D glasses, which hung by yarn from the cardboard. Like origami, paper money resembled doves, trees, loaves of bread, and fish from Galilee. When we got older, we recognized that the lighter the poster, the greater chance of winning. By eighth grade most of us just taped five dollars of baby-sitting money to a doily. That was the price of redeeming one pagan baby, five dollars. At least that's what Sister Marya had told us back in first grade, although I would imagine there has been some inflation over the years.

The grand prize was the relic of a saint encased between two pieces of clear plastic. A picture of the saint to whom the relic belonged was visible through one side of the plastic window and the relic on the other. The sides were sewn shut. If you wanted to wear it around your neck, a long piece of narrow grosgrain ribbon was slipped through a hole in the top of the plastic case. This was the most coveted prize at Saint Michael's grade school—to possess something that the saint had touched or aspired to touch. I thought for years that the relic was actually flesh—especially after one of the nuns said that if we no longer wanted to care for it, the relic needed a proper burial. I still have one.

Every Sunday we went to 10:00 mass, fasting from midnight forward to prepare to receive the body of Christ, topping it off with a fancy Sunday brunch. My father rarely came with us, preferring instead to stay home, filling his ashtray with Kents and his cup with coffee until breakfast was served around 11:15.

My mother hung a crucifix in each of our bedrooms, gave us icons of our namesakes and rosary beads in a rainbow of colors, my favorite being one that glowed in the dark. She placed a statue of Saint Christopher on the dashboard of our Chevy, prayed to Saint Anthony when something was lost, Saint Michael when someone died, and Saint Theresa of Avila for her migraines. When Mary was felled by spinal meningitis, polyneuritis, and encephalitis, my mother began a novena to Our Lady of Lourdes.

I am certain it was Labor Day weekend when the trilogy of diseases that infected my sister, Mary, became apparent. We were on our way back to the Boulevard from Big Fish Lake. The thirteen-hour car trip always made the three of us girls sick, but that day Mary developed a few nuanced symptoms beyond the usual nausea. No one really noticed anything particularly unusual until we stopped for our picnic lunch somewhere in Wisconsin, beyond the Dells, at the turnoff from Highway 12 where a Burma Shave sign fluttered in the traffic.

"A whiskey kiss for the one you adore
May not make her mad,
But her face will be sore."

Even though Mary read the rhyme with clear enough diction (she was an amazingly precocious reader) as she attempted to exit our Chevrolet Bel Air, she stumbled into one rear fin and literally hung there as if she were riding a dolphin. Mary could not be coaxed from her position and polio telegraphed between my parents. Polio.

I remember their look. It was one of terror.

The thimbleful of vaccine that we drank in the 1950s preceded a barrelful of admonitions regarding any type of public activity involving water—swimming, drinking, peeing. And as more photos of children in iron lungs were featured on the front page of newspapers, an equal number of myths arose. Mary's illnesses, however, were not from the lake water.

There were so many mosquitoes around the lake property that we almost became immune to the welts that rose on our bodies from their daily assault. Millions of insects swarmed the lake. Our outhouse, in particular, was inundated, as was the outdoor shower and the garbage pile at the back of the property by the dusty road. We had what mosquitoes wanted it would seem, along with succulent young flesh. In the woods where we cleaned fish and buried their carcasses, the mosquitoes whined around our bodies, taunting us, until we succumbed and slapped fish scales into the bite. Even with netting around our heads the insects were tenacious. There were warnings most summers—stay in after sundown, wear long sleeves, spray your body with DEET, eat garlic—but none were ever really heeded until Mary's case.

Visitors had to fight their way into Mary's room through a multitude of religious paraphernalia on the sunny fall afternoons after she came home from the hospital. There was a private font of holy water immediately to the right of the door, available upon entry. It was a small porcelain half-bowl attached to the wall with finishing nails. The little font, filled with blessed H2O, was barely big enough for the tips of the middle and index finger. But that was what visitors did, dipped into the font with their right hand to make a quick sign of the cross with their watery fingertips—forehead to sternum, left shoulder to the other. Holy water refills were obtained from a sterling silver flask stashed under Mary's bed. The font was removed and rinsed daily to prevent it from becoming the source of another viral outbreak.

Holy Cards were taped on the walls and a rosary dangled from the light switch. Scapulars made of two small pieces of cloth joined by strings were hung from the four posters of Mary's bed. Each supposedly had a healing power if the associated prayers were said as prescribed. A brown scapular of Our Lady of Mount Carmel promised that there would be no everlasting fire; another was sky blue and adorned with the symbol of the Immaculate Conception (sans genitalia). The red scapular of the Most Precious Blood pictured a chalice plus angels on its flip side. A black scapular featured the Blessed Virgin Mary under the title of "Help of the Sick" plus two helpmates—Camillus and Saint Joseph. The border was done in delicate cross-stitching. The scapulars were a cadre of colorful prescriptions and evidence of the deals made with God and Saint Jude Thaddeus. I have little doubt that my mother made her personal bargains with whomever of the spirits in the sky were listening: her life for Mary's. There was just something about the way she hummed around the sick room after a while, confident, really, that the outcome would be to her liking as long as she kept the scapulars hung and font filled. It was what I remembered shortly after her death, and then spent some time chastising myself for believing a god would make that kind of a trade, like a baseball card.

After my mother died, I found a pamphlet called *Confidence in God* lodged in her nightstand. I was a little surprised. After all, Mary had survived, prospered, really. It was inscribed on the inside front cover: *To Dorothy, from Mother, Easter 1962.* Filled with words of encouragement and admonitions to trust in God, it instructed the flailing faithful to concentrate on the present, leaving Him to worry about the future. I thought it good advice. If my mother had done just that, paid attention to *that day,* her last, she may have had a future. Unless God hadn't prepared one for her, which seemed dastardly considering the fallout. Which He knew would happen. He knows everything.

I read the pamphlet cover to cover and its message seemed onerous. It preached passivity, ill-advised in a marriage in which one person was already diminished. Was this gift from Mups an expression of concern that my mother was losing confidence in her life while trying to glean some from God?

I know for sure my mother served the *Marshall Field's Luncheon Sandwich*—cream cheese, mayonnaise, crabmeat, hard-boiled eggs on a Holland Rusk—with a slice of fruit pie, when she hosted her bridge group. Shortly after Mups presented her with a subscription to *Gourmet Magazine*, she began serving everything on a skewer—cheese and pineapple, mini- sausages, little corncobs alternating with marinated mushrooms and pickled onions, all of them *en brouchette*. The sticks were easily discarded; they were so mobile. Skewers littered the Hawthorne neighborhood. My mother moved on to toast points, slicing crusts from entire loaves and saving them in plastic bags for the birds at Morton's Arboretum in Chicago. There wasn't a foodstuff that couldn't somehow be served on a point. Plus, as my mother reminded us, toast points had that ability to be arranged in different patterns.

I found the recipe stuck in her copy of *The Joy of Cooking*. Her own handwriting lists the toppings.

Toast Points

One loaf, good quality, thin sliced white bread. Trim the crusts and slice in half on the diagonal, twice, to form four (4) triangles. Place the bread in a single layer on a baking sheet. Bake the bread in a preheated 425 degree oven for 4-5 minutes, checking to make sure it doesn't become too dark. Turn and bake on the other side, 2-3 minutes. Cool the "points" on a baking rack.

Toppings

1. *Sterling caviar topped with crème fraiche*
2. *Tomato and kalamata olives with smoked salmon*
3. *Pink Triangle Nova Lox*
4. *Pickled jellyfish*
5. *Smoked trout dip*
6. *Finnan Haddie and artichokes*
7. *Duckling with Apple Jack Brandy Sauce*

8. Shrimp with lemon cream sauce

9. Foi Gras

10. Crab, parsley, cream cheese, horseradish, mustard, onion

11. Cream cheese with walnuts

12. Cucumber, lettuce, mayo

13. Welsh rarebit

14. Individual ham rounds with eggs

15. Scallops, white wine, parmesan cheese

16. Creamed eggs

17. Chicken salad with cashews

18. Baked brie

19. Warm brandy and wild mushroom pate

20. Fluffer-nutter

I also know she spent time as a volunteer in the Women's Assistance League selling white elephants, was a member of the Infant Children's Welfare Society of Illinois, and volunteered to serve lunch at Saint Michael's Grade School on Hot Dog Day. Her last meeting before she died was attending the Saint Francis High School Mother's Club. I wonder what activities they accomplished that evening? A vote on the Spring Musical? Planning senior night or the faculty-staff appreciation event? Perhaps her last assignment was a note thanking someone for the rolled cookies that were donated for the parent meeting. She would have been into hospitality.

Dear Nancy,
The sugar cookies were delicious. Thank you so much for your generous donation of time. I would love the recipe!
Sincerely,
Dorothy

Would Nancy have already penned the recipe on a three-by-five card when she read the obituary a week later? "Dorothy Donnelly, suddenly, Jan. 20, 1963…"

Would it have been better if her life had been defined by something other than her *sudden* death? If she had a terminal illness, would we have talked about her energy in the face of chemo, drugs, or surgery? Would we have admired her strength and courage even though her illness was formidable? Would she have had the inclination to whisper that I, or Patty, or Mary was her favorite (don't tell the others!), that she admired a special talent in each of us? Maybe she would have taped a message, or a favorite bedtime story to transition us into motherlessness on those first lonely nights. Or perhaps she would have preferred a personal letter written in her loose script. But the fact remains, she never had to face the prospect of reorganizing her priorities, making amends, accomplishing a goal (quickly now!), or asking for a syringe filled with medicine to end it all. She probably didn't even have a moment to review her life or retrieve one memory to hold tight as she lay on the floor. It was, after all, *sudden*.

I inherit a box of loose photographs from the Boulevard. I balance it on my lap as I write this, and greedily examine the prints containing my mother's face, waiting for some memories to surface, waiting for something I know for sure. About her.

My fingers brush across her brow, as if they might read information lost to my consciousness. My mind stalls. Any thoughts that lie on the edge quickly become subsumed within the memory of that night, stagnant from speculation.

I stare at the backs of old photos where my father once made notes of names and dates. I close my eyes and imagine the precision with which he executed his manuscript, blue ink flowing from his cherished pen, the lettering minute, slanted slightly to the left, each letter the same height as the one before, lined as if a ruler provided some support. *'Daint' February 15, 1947.* The date of their wedding. *'Daint' September, 1947.* Patty arrives! *'Daint' May, 1949.* My christening. *'Daint' at the Lake*, until 1962, with Mary and Patty, Mups and me. This attention to detail provides an antidote to my anxiety for a moment; the secret slightly diminished in the protective shadow of his hand.

I can only imagine this nickname came about because of her wasp-like waist, and strikingly small hands and feet, her narrow shoulders, and small stature. I squint at the last photo of her life. It was developed two months after her death, March 1963. She is wearing a short black wool coat with a mink collar and black leather gloves. Her calves look slim as she stands in high heels even though it is snowy. Her hair is in a French twist. Her face looks bloated, her smile tight. She is unaware that death is staring back at her through the lens of the camera. If only I had the negative. Maybe I could coax more information from the slippery celluloid.

I look for hints in the photographs that may have foreshadowed her early demise. There is one of her lying on a rubber raft in Big Fish Lake. Her hands are stroking the water. She is young and slim, her brunette hair tied back. She looks unflinchingly at the camera and her dimples are deep on either side of her broad mouth. Her figure is swathed in a one-piece suit and she looks happy. I wonder now who snapped the shot. Was it my father positioning the lens, saying, "Smile for me Dot? Show me a little cleavage! Come on, smile for the camera." She looks like she is enjoying the attention. I want to believe my father felt lucky right then. But what I crave to know is if he admired her. I search for stories that he may have told us—stories that I may have forgotten. I ask my sisters. I try to jumpstart their memory. But no one has any information.

There is another—a photo of two handsome couples lounging on a picnic blanket—my mother and father, his brother and wife. The women are wearing dresses cinched at their waists, and high heels. The men have thick heads of hair combed back, strong bodies, lean and fluid. Their smiles are broad but guarded. They have a proprietary air about them. They look proud, snuggling close to their wives. My father hasn't written a caption on this one so I print, "Tom with the love of his life," mimicking his script.

The picture of my mother that I treasure the most, though, is one of her in a nursing uniform showing her now-famous narrow waist, plump soft lips, and head of thick brunette hair. She was all teeth and bosom. Her posture implies good health. She doesn't look over-whelmed as happened later on when her buxomness became ordinary and matronly; when in her thirties her shoulders became dented and waist became engulfed in a layer of fat; when her slender arms became a reflective image of languid muscle hanging below; and thighs, once so shapely, became cumbersome and riddled with varicosities. There was some speculation after she died that perhaps all this fattening was a sort of prodromal warning that she wasn't well, that perhaps her uterus needed removing. It sounds strange now, but as a child I remember there being some discussion about her uterus and weight gain; that at one point she had to reposition her organ after it fell into her undies. (For a time I developed an unrealistic image of wombs, imagining them as something that might drag behind me on an elastic chord.)

When I try to decipher the memories etched in my heart, they seem mundane. A picture emerges without substance, without passion. I see her in terms of things through a fog of uncertainty.

Would she have lived in a trailer? (I developed an affinity for Airstream trailers as a child. A portable house. A slender silver marshmallow! Pick up and go. Did this come from her? Or from the movie, *The Long, Long Trailer,* with Lucille Ball? One of my favorites. Did she like that movie? Or any movie?) I don't think she had any wanderlust, although I'm unsure if she ever had the opportunity presented to her, except for Big Fish Lake, of course.

I think she despised gum chewing and whistling. She was impeccable in her housekeeping. She liked baths and perfume. And even though I don't know this for sure, I would bet her underwear was always clean, without holes or tears. I think she liked Milton Berle, was jealous of Donna Reed, and disapproved of my infatuation with Annie Oakley. She made me hang my holster on a nail in the garage after my revolver scratched a coffee table. She trimmed the plastic fringe on my western skirt to clean the dirty ends. When I started kindergarten, she dressed me in a yellow dotted swiss dress with a set of crinolines and tight patent shoes. She insisted I would survive the afternoon without my "get-up." I got a rash. My mother said it was psychosomatic.

"Remember when you thought your arm was pulled out of the socket when your father was swinging you like an airplane? You wouldn't move it for over a week. You carried it around in a white dishtowel shaped like a sling. We were convinced that your alter ego had gotten you into some kind of battle. You are wearing dresses to school."

I hid my boots under a dogwood on the way to school and traded places with my shiny Mary Jane's, permanently spotted after sustaining a day of lawn watering.

Her senior biography written in the yearbook of Lyons Township High School in 1943 says she had a "nifty smile and winning personality"; she had "friends galore" and could be seen "cutting a rug" at a place called Vann's with a boy named Roy. The bio also states that she wanted to enter nurse's training, which she did, graduating from Loyola University School of Nursing in 1946. I have her yearbook photos from 1940 through 1943, all with the same smile, the same brunette hair, cardigan sweaters, and a string of pearls.

I read a prayer from the Mass of Saint Basil and organize the last set of photographs. It is their wedding day. This is the Mass she selected. I look at my mother's folded hands and imagine she is whispering the prayer of *The Good Shepherd.*

The Lord is my shepherd. I shall lack nothing.
He has taken me to green pastures,
He has led me to still waters;
He has healed my spirit.
He has led me along right paths
For his own name's sake.
Even if I walk in the valley of the shadow of death,
I shall fear no evil, for you are with me:
Your rod and your staff give me comfort...

In the wedding photos, she is wearing a white chiffon and satin gown with seed pearls. Her skirt falls to the floor, billowy with crinoline, Patty snug in her womb. She holds a bouquet of stephanotis, white roses, and orchids. On her head is a cap of lilies of the valley from which her veil tumbles to her shoulders in tiers. My grandfather looks uncomfortable standing in the back of the church, my mother's arm linked through his. Her mouth is open a little, as if she is surprised to be there. Half-way down the aisle, she meets my father, who turns a bit towards her, a smile playing around his lips. Her head is bowed and I detect she is smiling too. Before they leave the church they listen to Panis Angelicus, and Gounod's Ave Maria. I listen too, pleased that I have something in my repertoire that she may have chosen. A shiny black sedan sits in front of Saint Francis Xavier as the couple emerges, my father holding my mother's arm. The car pulls away as white streamers flutter behind them.

My last recollection of my mother alive was on the night she died. We were facing each other across a yard of snow. I was in the home of our neighbor, the doctor, who would be the same man a few hours later pronouncing her dead. She was standing on our side patio watching my younger sister make her way through the cold toward me. I was to watch Mary as well. My mother was smiling. She flicked the porch light off and on, stood still for a moment and waved. I saw her red lips break into a smile. This time I waved back and opened the door, gathering Mary into my arms.

I don't remember my mother's voice. I don't remember a certain kiss or way of hugging. If she told me my own birth story, it eludes me. I can't remember daily rituals, favorite sayings, ways of being. We never had a favorite game or secret language. If she read to me I cannot recall. My mind draws a blank when I try to think of one little quirk that belonged only to her. I marvel at books that are written entirely about mothers. I think there is something wrong with a person to hold so few memories, that I must be constipated with fear.

I try to imagine my mother in her seventies. Her hair is silver and thick. Her complexion looks translucent even under the brush of age. Her figure is lush. I collect older friends and examine their every nuance. I am watchful of their interaction with their children.

I stand on the sidelines and imagine they belong to me. That I am their child. I am a voyeur. I can't help myself.

I invent names at night as my brain chatters its way into the underworld, names defining a long life. I imagine I hear my own children calling for her, their grandmother. "Hey Grandma Dainty Dot," "Grandma Dot," "Grams Dot," "Dotty Gram," or "Grandma Jean Josephine," they shout, wrapping their arms around her soft swollen belly. We would have been silly like that. Or creative, giving her gifts that were polka-dotted with tags which read "To: Nana Dots."

My sisters and I stand together in front of a mirror. We see her smile, even down to the small overbite which inevitably catches a swipe of red lipstick no matter the blotting. We walk in her petite steps and relish the same attention to detail. We search antique stores for hat pins and elbow length gloves. We buy strands of rhinestones, brooches with art deco motifs, handbags that smell like loose tobacco, dresses with full skirts and cinched waists, hats with perky veils that graze our eyebrows. We search for her in discarded mementoes from the life of someone we don't know. We put her together in a montage of pieces. We wait for her face to stare back at us.

I want to believe my mother would have described me as beloved and faithful; that she would have seen me as honest and charitable. I imagine that she would have sung to me the Irish Love Song, "Bride at Fourteen, My Sweet Mauvorneen." It would have been our secret.

O, you plant the pain in my heart with your wistful eyes,
Girl of my choice, Maureen!
Will you drive me mad for the kisses your shy
sweet mouth denies,
Maureen?

Like a walking ghost I am, and no words to woo,
White rose of the West, Maureen;
For it's pale you are and the fear that's on you is

over me too,
Maureen!

Sure it's our complaint that's on us, asthore, this day,
Bride of my dreams, Maureen;
The smart of the bee that stings us, his honey
must cure they say,
Maureen!

I'll coax the light to your eyes, and the rose to your face,
Mavourneen, my own Maureen,
When I feel the warmth of your breast, and your
nest is my arm's embrace,
Maureen!

O where was the King of the World that day—only me,
My one true love, Maureen.
And you the Queen with me there, and your
throne in my heart, machree,
Maureen!

Sometimes I pretend I can hear her whisper, "I love you my sweet Mavourneen."

Chapter 5

Mups and Mom...
and Gramps

My memory sweeps over thirteen years of sunny summers observing Mups and Mom and their devoted relationship to one another. Wherever I look, there they are, pressed into each other in a conspiratorial fashion. I was vaguely jealous at those moments, yet instinctively knew I was ill-prepared right then for the selflessness befitting a close to perfect rapport. Unfortunately their circle never wound around to full, including us, my sisters and me, within this instructive loop. And while my mother's early death released her from some of the unhealthier family traits—arthritis and gallstones, and yes, the creeping obsequiousness like an indomitable cancer, it denied her access to the full complement of *our* love, a largess eventually curdled by melancholy.

As much as I try to disinter details about my mother, it is always Mups who blooms full-formed in her stead. Mups , the quintessential teacher of everything proper—posture, propriety, table manners, white gloves, hats in church, lipstick, clean-shaven underarms, modest bathing suits, hosiery, one-inch heels, daily rosary, weekly communion. And while the three of us adored her, some of her lessons could have proved fatal (how much weight could we *possibly* lose to please her?). I think of her now as a healthy neurotic with poetic tendencies. She was a comedienne. In my mind she had many signs of anorexia, although she seemed a particularly adventuresome cook with her roulades, ratatouilles, and cream sauces. (I could spell everyone!) In fact Mups was so tall and thin that she bragged about losing her panties at a baseball game. They just slid right off her hips, she said. It happened somewhere around home plate, when she was performing a particularly complicated cheer and a button popped on the waistband.

"There I was with my panties around my ankles and my arms in the air," she told us. "I just stepped out of them and scooped them into my purse in a flash. I never stopped cheering."

"I'll bet she adjusted her high kicks, though," Patty whispered.

Mups had journals filled with song lyrics, poems, and sayings. Sometimes she would repeat the more nonsensical ones over and over. "*Flat foot floogee with the floy floy, flat foot floogee with the floy, floy, flat foot floogee with the floy, floy, floy doy, floy doy, floy doy, floy doy.*"

If she had a failing it was only that she would abduct her favorite lines from some dead poet like Walt Whitman to mix with another, equally dead. "Oh captain! my captain, our fearful trip is done. The ship has weather'd every rack, the prize we sought is won…" (Whitman). "Oh east is east, and west is west, and never the twain shall meet, till earth and sky stand presently at God's great judgment seat…" (Kipling).

If she had a further weakness, it was that she was a contortionist with words—hers, theirs, someone's, anyone's. (What's plagiarism, Grandma?)

But all was forgiven when Mups recited her silly rhymes, word for word, although I remain unsure of their origin!

Last night I held a little hand,
So dainty and so sweet.
I thought my heart would burst with joy
So wildly did it beat.
I pressed it gently to my heart, and
Cared not for another thing, than

That little hand I held last night
4 Aces and a King.

(Mups Kost, 1918, private)

I never sensed Mom and Mups were rivals. I don't recall a conversation in which my mother disparaged Mups, her child-rearing,
fashion, or quirkiness. Nor do I have a memory that Mups was
blamed for caring too much or too little—which seems to be almost
a rite of passage with some daughters. They bought the same knit
suits, played bridge, smoked, drank, and shared a dry sense of humor. They married similar men. I am almost certain they both used
sedatives, Miltowns, "Mickey Finns" they were called when mixed
with alcohol. Both women were prone to lectures, which lost their
punch midstream from the monotony. They loved wetland birds like
the Great Blue Heron, deep-fried frog legs, yams, thick jams, strong
coffee, dark bread, and canned beets. They made the best bean soup
by simmering a hambone in the bottom of a pressure cooker until
the meat floated to the top. In fact, when I picture them together they
melt into one another, sitting shoulder to shoulder in crisp white
sleeveless shirts tied up at their midriff. They are snapping beans
and shucking corn, rolling pie crust and breading fish, sitting at the
picnic table on the long porch of Mups' cottage. If it were possible,
they would have shared the same fingerprint.

The only discernible differences that I can recall between them
was, first, their preference for cocktails—my grandmother loved a
highball while my mother enjoyed the Perfect Manhattan; and second, the detail with which their separate bars were assembled.

We had shelves of accouterments for drink-making in Wheaton:
double-sided jiggers, cocktail pitchers—one stainless steel, the other heavy glass with drink recipes etched on the sides, a Hawthorne
strainer, stir sticks made of glass and metal, with one in sterling silver,
which was retractable to a convenient travel size. There were shelves
of glistening glassware—short for single malts and highballs, even
shorter for after-dinner liqueurs, and tall glassware when the season

called for a Tom Collins, or a vodka tonic. There was stemware for martinis, Manhattans, champagne, and the rare aperitif.

Below the glasses was an enclosed liquor cabinet, locked in fact, with four or five shelves of crème de cacao, bourbon, Jim Beam, Canadian Club, Gordon's Gin, Russian vodka, dark and light rum, tequila, peppermint schnapps, mixers, chasers, and ingredients for a "little hair of the dog," the closest we ever came to having a pet. Reading all those labels and surmising the origin of the mixtures was a veritable geography lesson. Bottles of varying sizes sat on the edge of a glass shelf with reinforcements stacked behind, the labels all facing to the front, carefully dusted.

My parents drank every night from the same Manhattan glasses etched with a 'D', both sitting in identical chairs on Hawthorne Boulevard, separated by a cocktail table. (My parents maintained the same cocktail hour ritual at the lake, only they dispensed with the formal bartending amenities and drank from tumblers. They sat in a secluded corner of the front yard or shared the hour with Mups and Gramps, alternating between the cottages, although the latter sometimes disintegrated into a shouting match between the men.)

We began stirring Perfect Manhattans for our parents at about the same time we donned training bras. It became a rite of passage: swizzle stick passed from the eldest down through the ranks at the same time our protuberances were being protected for future padding and underwire. By the time the swizzle stick reached Mary, our mother was dead.

In order for the Perfect Manhattan to take on its characteristic mahogany color, precise measurement was necessary: equal parts of sweet and dry vermouth with twice as much bourbon, ice cubes for chilling purposes only. In fact the alcohol in the first batch only tickled the ice briefly—long enough to cool but not dilute. The red maraschino stationed at the bottom of the glass, stem pointed upward, was vibrant and alive, as was my father. The first batch of Perfect Manhattans actually civilized the man, although we never really understood to what extent until after our mother died. (On weekends, in her absence, there was only a brief window of time when my father was civil—between 10:30 and 4:30, post-hangover to pre-drunk.)

Only after my mother died were we allowed into the living room for cocktail hour carte blanche. At first, none of us could bear the thought of our father sitting there ticking off the hour. We sat on the gold shag circling his feet, picking at the loops, carefully avoiding our mother's chair, or her name, or comments that would allude to the necessity of our ever *needing* a mother. We sat through the first batch and as quickly as his charm left the room, so did we. When he wanted more, he merely picked up the shaker and shook the remaining ice cubes.

"Clink, clink, clink." Three only. Quick. The deftness of his wrist spoke to us.

"Three parts to one, make it equal and fine. Fifty quick stirs and it will be considered sublime."

That's what we chanted—stir the liquid exactly fifty times (as per father's instructions), counting aloud by ones if he was nearby and if not, then by twos, and if you dared, by threes, leaving the remainders unstirred.

This second batch of Manhattans was dubbed the "Lessthanperfect" Manhattan. The color looked like tea, but the blend of liquors could still fool the numbed taste buds. The maraschino, a little plumper now, rocked unsteadily, its stem almost perpendicular to the bottom of the glass. If we were very unlucky, the pitcher clinked a third time. This batch took its color from the cubes that lay melting in the bottom of the three-shake-night. Only a little water was added, maybe a new maraschino, the old one looking pinkish and bloated, a bleached old fruit calling too much attention to this aberration called the Perfect Manhattan. It was a rhythm we acquired, a dancing flotilla of prepubescent girls, sliding in and out of the room to the beat of the clinking, measuring, pouring, stirring.

I wondered later how Mups survived the death of her daughter. I only remember her stoicism when she entered the front hall of our home in Wheaton the day after my mother died. She wore her fox stole with its head and tail nipping at each other as it lay across her shoulders. Her skirt was straight and black and she wore a hat with a small veil covering her eyes. Before she went to my parents' bedroom, she removed her gloves, and then lifted her veil. I remember her hands were shaking. The bedroom had already been scrubbed, double Dutch clean (except for the stain by the side of the bed), but she went to stare anyway, and like all those wreaths laid by the side of the road from accidents in Minnesota, she probably wanted to do the same. (God's will, Mups.)

It is with some sense of bitterness that I reflect upon my grandmother's accident five years later which rendered her incapacitated, a minute short of death. Our wonderful Mups, who I want to think loved us unconditionally, and *worried* about the remnants of our childhood, how we were being parented, and if we were being nurtured. But I am unsure if she really tried to advocate for us, to step into a situation that clearly wasn't going well. Maybe she didn't know about my slipping grades, the cocktail parties hosted by Patty on Hawthorne Boulevard while my father traveled, the couples that I had to kick out of my bed on those nights, locking my door, trying to sleep as the party pressed on. Or that her daughter Shirley had to buy me a winter coat, one whose cost my father flatly refused to reimburse on the grounds that it was too expensive. Too fancy. "I didn't approve this!" he told her. It was from *Lord and Taylor* and sported too many gold buttons. "And epaulets, for Christ's sake," he spat! And if she recognized the extremes of our grief—Patty's hyper-exuberance, my isolation, and Mary's ... She didn't interfere. The only time Mups insisted on interjecting herself into my life was after I started to "puff up"; a sign of self-indulgence rather than an emotional upheaval.

As luck would have it, I was house sitting for them the weekend of the accident, in Omaha, where I was attending college. They were on their way to Chicago, to attend Mary's graduation from eighth grade. Grandma was looking forward to the trip on the Burlington

Zephyr, first class, sleeping berths, and dinner on white linen served by "the nicest black porters you ever saw," she told me. "They always wear white gloves and carry a white linen cloth draped over their arms. They never touch anything with their bare hands, those boys, nothing that would dare touch your lips."

When I say it was luck that I happened to be at their home that morning, the implication is not that I wished Mups to become irreparably broken, but rather that I was an eyewitness to the events—almost. After grandma died, a cousin in the family intimated that Grandpa probably tried to kill Mups—not such an absurd supposition, and one that I entertained briefly until it became unbearable to imagine the lives of these two women to be that similar.

Grandma was injured by a light fixture which fell from the kitchen ceiling nicking the back of her neck with the most delicate of incisions. Mups would have liked that, the precision of the slice, but as it turned out, she never quite grasped the gravity of her predicament. Admittedly I was not actually *in* the kitchen (not again!) when the globe fell to the floor, but I found it hard to imagine Gramps, who had changed a light bulb the day before, purposely and precisely aligned the three screws in such a way that they would release the glass globe at the exact moment Grandma paused beneath to fetch some crullers from the breadbox. (Or if he did, maybe it was intended for me!) Perhaps my cousin heard the same rumor as I, the one where Grandpa threw a carving knife at Mups. Apparently it landed squarely in their cutting board. Did Mups duck? Was this some sort of circus act? (Mups and Gramps, renowned knife thrower and assistant from Nebraska, show their skill with common kitchen cutlery.) I wasn't particularly alarmed with the story. I guess I was used to having knives as weapons around in Wheaton. My father kept an old hunting knife on the top shelf of his closet, on the right side, behind a brown leather satchel. Its rusty nicked blade lay tucked into its own leather sheath with a tight snap around the handle. My sisters and I examined it for remnants of blood only once. Patty was the one that actually held the knife, unsnapping the wrapper, extracting it by the handle and giggling excitedly about how heavy it was. She had donned a pair of elbow-length gloves for the occasion, so as not to leave any prints, "like Lizzie Borden," I remember she said. She made me a little nervous. After that we never touched it again but checked regularly, making sure it hadn't been moved. As far as my grandfather was concerned, though, he had a history which was suspect. Perhaps my cousin was right, the knife-throwing incident was foreshadowing.

(Gramps *was* an intemperate man. He had a reputation for excessive behavior. He was as exploitive as Mups was sincere. Gramps was explosive. Corrosive. Everybody paled when he was around and tried to live under his radar. There was something about Gramps that lay just under the surface of his self-satisfaction that was threatening.)

When my grandfather entered the guestroom where I was sleeping the morning of Grandma's accident, it was very early, maybe around 5:00 a.m. We had said our goodbyes the night before, so I was startled when he stood over me and said that Grandma had a bit of an accident. It sounded very familiar.

("Wake up!" he whispers into my ear. "Grandma's had an accident. Pray. If you have never prayed before, do now.")

From the look of the amount of blood that had spattered across the kitchen cabinets, the floor, and walls, and my favorite sweet rolls sitting on the counter, I imagined Mups had cut a pretty important connector. She sat between us in the front seat of their gold Cadillac as we sped towards the hospital, listing towards my chest, holding a cold compress to her wound. Her beautiful purple suit had dark splotches down the front placket. When I looked down at my own clothing, it was soaked with red. I started to get dizzy waiting for the few thousand spots floating in front of my eyes to dissipate, while Mups, quite calmly, announced to Gramps that she couldn't see anymore. "Ray," Mups whispered, "I am blind." As simple as that, she snapped us all to attention. Gramps started sucking on a nitroglycerine tablet.

The hospital personnel wasted a few precious moments at first, focusing on my bloodstained pajama top, urging me to lie on a stretcher. "Where is the injury?" they asked as they probed my chest looking for a wound. "Were you shot?"

"I'm blind," Mups said again, still standing, still applying pressure to her neck. "Just a minute, dear," one of the nurses said absently to Grandma. "I know you're blind."

Then Mups passed out.

Weeks later, she emerged from a coma atrophied into a twist that affected her right side. In the course of his guilt, Gramps became the ultimate pragmatist, retiring from consulting work, outfitting her chair with a tray for meals, and purchasing a van with a hydraulic lift. Her hospital bed was motorized as well and sported mobiles of absurd characters set to music for visual stimulation. Mups would sit for hours in her wheelchair, head lolling forward, sometimes letting it rest on her tray. Her eyes were damp, drool and bubbles leaked from the side of her mouth, and urine from her catheter.

It took some time, but we knew Mups was on the mend when she recited one of her favorite poems, maybe not perfectly, but that was always true.

The meeting it was sudden
As well as it was sad.
She sacrificed her own sweet life
The only one she had.
The daisies on the hillside are lying o'er her now
For that is what will happen
When a freight train meets a cow.

Gramps was renewed. He rushed around her in frenzied activity—bathing, feeding, toileting, combing her hair straight back and attaching bright plastic barrettes, usually pink and in the shape of bows or hearts. He applied her lipstick in two straight red lines and rouge in perfect circles on each cheek. He positioned a whistle around her neck, which Mups learned to blow shrilly for his attention. She wore nighties most of the time, except when Gramps took her to Jerry's Supper Club in Richmond, Minnesota. Then Mups wore a dress with her stole draped across her lap, the fox head clipping the spokes of her chair. She came to love Perfect Manhattans, and her catheter bag would grow dark with whiskey each evening as she grew melancholic. Sometimes she called for my mother.

I don't know how my grandfather treated my mother. Even after observing Gramps care for Mups, my memory remains uninformed. I am especially unsettled over this lack of information because I suspect she was fearful of him, and I wonder if she married this feeling—of fear. I don't remember them having a conversation, sharing a hug, a kiss in greeting, a certain respect. When I asked Patty what she remembered, only one thing stood out. "He called her fat," she said with contempt. (This was the ultimate insult in my family.) But the word *fear* lurks nearby even now. Holes in her history loom large when I try inserting Gramps. Their story, unlike the one with Mups, has the girth of a strand of hair, held together by only one substantial fact—his Last Will and Testament.

I found a photo of my grandfather, with my mother's arm slipped through his, both of them mugging for the camera, enjoying the graduation of my mother's brother from law school. Yet, this would be the brother who would act as attorney for Gramps as he drafted his Last Will and Testament, his last wish for his family, which successfully eliminated our mother from the family tree and therefore her progeny—us! The three girls! (There he stood, freshly scrubbed in the law! Where was Mups' crystal ball?) In short, his will divided the estate equally among only three of his four children.

I study him, Gramps, his hair slicked back with oil, looking slightly vulnerable. He is wearing a striped tie and dark suit. I can almost hear him laughing, the laugh that he could never control when something took him by surprise. My mother is smiling broadly too, perhaps laughing, although I can't remember what it sounded like. They look like a loving family at that moment, except I know the vindictiveness which is lying fertile in my grandfather's gut and how he will so carefully construct his last words with his son as scrivener.

I think Gramps utilized his Last Will and Testament to retaliate against my father, the man he neither liked nor respected, and who, above all, outlived his daughter. My father was the only spouse mentioned in the will as being able to provide for his children, thus explaining, it would seem, my grandfather's departure from the *normal* will. (A predeceased child such as my mother is usually included in such document, with her portion of the estate distributed to any children. This did not happen.) Yet, Uncle Tom, the lawyer, and Uncle Bob, the Chevy dealer and Aunt Shirley's husband, were wealthy men, able to provide for their children, as well. In fact both were better situated than my father financially and emotionally. Gramps knew that. But he had a point to make, and in doing so he ultimately destroyed a family.

I thought for certain one of my mother's sisters or brother would intervene, making this malevolence unsuccessful. But again, the very opposite happened. The lines of communication were shut down between her three siblings and us after we asked why Gramps did this, treating us unlike his other grandchildren, and our mother, unlike his other children. We asked Tommy, the lawyer, my mother's brother. He assumed we were after money and simply unable to understand that, *to us*, the will was symbolic. That something bigger than money was involved. Uncle Tommy did not respond as one who appreciated our loss. Nor did my mother's two sisters.

I try to propose some rationale besides money for this abandonment by my mother's family of origin, which continued to their deaths. (What is this menu of anger and contempt of which her family partakes? Its longevity, over thirty years, must provide the nourishment to sustain such small mindedness. Such enmity. Is heartlessness genetic? Would my mother have done the same?) Perhaps because we didn't desert our father, the family felt we had rejected their sister, Dorothy, our mother. To them, this may have been unforgiveable. But of course, I lived the destructiveness of this quandary—being open with what I knew about the death and the implications this information would proffer; or protecting the secret. And thus my father.

But whatever the reason for their shunning, Gramps gave them permission to behave as if we weren't bona fide members of the family tree by treating us differently. And Patty, Mary, and I gave them justification when we asked, "Why?" After that, I had moments when I wondered if my mother ever existed at all. I wondered if her siblings, Pat or Tommy, or her best friend, Shirley, ever spoke of her. Or if Gramps had been successful in erasing whatever narrative my mother had accrued over her thirty-seven years by completing his own.

My memories of Gramps are mostly from the lake, before the will, where he would engage in frenetic activity—painting, reroofing, sodding, seeding, and raking rocks that washed to shore every night. (Rake, throw, rake, throw, rake, rake, rake. Grimace.) Every morning! Was it mania or meditation?) Sometimes he abandoned the lake bottom for the gully which separated his cottage from the one next door that would eventually become ours. There he would help rake decades of leaves into a huge pile to later set on fire. He didn't pay particular attention to the glowing ash either, which stayed hot at the bottom of the pile days after the fire as my cousins and I played and ran through the soft embers. I got burned one year, running barefoot through the gulley. Too afraid to confess as blisters raised themselves from my foot, I soaked them in the lake. (Were the lake gods muttering "stupe"?)

Aunt Wee Wee, who was visiting the lake that summer, noticed my limp as we were climbing the hill to the Grasshopper Assumption Chapel. It was a landmark in the area, close to the lake, and dedicated to the BVM for saving the area crops from locusts. After a phalanx of prayer was dispatched from the countryside, the Blessed Virgin promptly responded with a snowstorm. The insects were destroyed. She was honored with this chapel, the Grasshopper Chapel, and a shrine with a granite kneeler below her beatific smile and outstretched hands. Unfortunately a tornado hit the chapel seven years later. All that remained was a tree which was gnarled into an unimaginable form unless you were prone to nightmares. This was where I was slumped when Aunt Wee Wee asked me what was wrong.

"Y-Y-Y- have to t-t-tell your m-m-m-m-m-," she said.

"I can't Aunt Wee Wee. I can't tell my mother. She will tell my father."

(Who will tell Sister and I will have more tests!)

The story morphed into a conflagration of events which posited me, the erstwhile dunce, who at the age of ten ran through flames! And lived! (A walking Dante's Inferno.) Mercilessly, my father taunted me with his own details of how my injury happened and added the story to his cocktail conversations. For some reason, he preferred to be entertained by my errors in judgment, rather than assessing any adult culpability.

"Hey kids," Gramps shouts, waving his rake. "Stay out of the gully until I have a chance to rake these embers into the dirt."

As his need for constant motion was satiated, Gramps would rest by donning a lopsided straw hat decorated with lures, grabbing his box of oils. Then he would set up an easel by the side of the gulley and paint the same scene over and over again—the lake property with trees a little too green, a sky too blue, and birds too bloated. With his free hand, Gramps would reach behind him towards his stool, grabbing a handful of chocolate covered crèmes to shovel in his mouth. When the candy box emptied, the landscape was completed.

He drank everything in gulps, his coffee in the morning, beer in the afternoon, scotch on the rocks towards nightfall. When he smoked, which was rare, he burned holes in his polyester Sansabelts. He laughed in short bursts baring his teeth like a horse usually passing gas mid-sentence. And he swore profusely, especially when he enlisted me to pull his nose hairs. "Come here, Peanut!" he'd yell to me. "Say, pull a few of these, will ya?" Which I would, tentatively at first, just grabbing the end of a hair with Grandma's tweezers, nursing it from his nostril. It must have been torturous for those few seconds because Gramps would suddenly arch his head backwards

putting his scratchy hand over mine to yank out a gray clump himself. "Like this, dammit," he'd scream. "Quit telling me about blood
clots! I don't give a good goddam, Peanut. Just pull."

Gramps scared me.

He loved taking us to Saint Cloud, the biggest city close to the
lake, one with a touch of sophistication, according to Mups. "Maybe
it's because of the Mississippi River that people are so genteel. Are
you aware it was named after a Paris suburb?" she would ask every
time. (Tom Sawyer meets Flaubert!) He took us to a meat packing
plant there, where my sisters and I would slide our shoes into white
paper slippers, our heads into loose hard hats, only to accompany a
steer who, unfortunately, we had named before it was hit with a stun
gun. How fast it was that robust good health could be stripped away,
along with fur and flesh and entrails until a glistening slab of blood-
soaked meat hung from a mighty hook! (Was Gramps trying to illustrate the tenuousness of life?) A river of blood flowed into drains as
men pushed the liquid with long brooms followed by a steady spray
of water. We were quiet during the slaughter, eagerly waiting to toss
our paper clothes into bins at the exit. Gramps would then herd us to
a hamburger joint to celebrate the experience.

He presented us with lake pets, a goose named Buster and an old
box turtle named Herb. Herb ended up with his shell nailed to an
old tree right by the front door where his innards were yanked out,
barely a morsel, and tossed into a pot of soup stock. His shell was
painted green to match the trim on my grandparents' cottage and
shellacked for an ashtray. Buster was basted to a golden brown and
served alongside a medley of fresh veggies washed by our tears.

There was a kind of carelessness with the lives of these crea-
tures. A pecking order. Endurance of the fittest. Alpha male. I didn't
learn survival skills as much as how power could be abused. (Okay,
it was just a turtle. But where were Mups and Mom? They disappear from these scenes time and time again. Is that what I was
being taught?)

I learned to scrutinize faces, gestures, and words, especially the roar of silence which propelled me from them, Dad, or Gramps, and toward a chore if the static in the air threw sparks. You could count on being left alone if your industry somehow benefitted these men. Raking, weeding, sweeping cobwebs, throwing rocks, painting, digging for bait kept them at bay, and you, invisible.

But what we weren't taught was how to live after the queen of all disasters. How to break apart the nut of grief and quell the ferocity of desperation. How to live with loneliness and unanswered questions. How to find love and meaning. (Wasn't there one person who thought it reparative to hug, rock, or soothe us just a bit?) But there we were, wisps of girls, myself barely recognizable through the bloated secret, trying to make sense of our lives, daring to breach the boundaries of our own experiences, looking for some sort of guidance, just a little nudge in the right direction.

Chapter 6
The Furies

Each summer, at least once, a storm would arrive at the lake like a belligerent guest, staying only long enough to remind us that we were the ones uninvited. The storm during the summer of 1962 would be my mother's last. It was ferocious. Patty and I were rowing around the lake in my grandfather's fishing boat, a heavy thing made of wood with three seats, painted evergreen on the outside and varnished to a sheen on the inside. We were sitting side by side in the middle seat, sliding a little from the baby oil on our legs, each gripping an oar. My grandfather wasn't at the lake that week. In fact there were no adult males around on the day of this storm. My mother, her two sisters, and Mups were lolling in beach chairs they had placed in the shallow water. They wore tennis shoes to protect their feet from the rocks that had washed to shore the night before, and their short, ruffled skirts undulated around them like four jellyfish.

The boat was motorless for the time being. My grandfather's three HP Evinrude trolling motor had snapped its safety chain the summer before and was sitting somewhere in the bottom of the lake. Unfortunately this had occurred when I was taking my maiden voyage as sole occupant and captain of his boat. My extended family had been lined up on the dock, the adults with their cocktails, children with miniature flags, to bid me farewell and Godspeed, something of a tradition for those of us who were celebrating their twelfth birthday.

I had primed the motor, yanked the starter rope, cranked the speed dial from idle to medium, and in a burst of exhilaration, noise, and exhaust fumes, the motor vanished. *Voila!* I remember thinking.

The motor had been loose all along on the boat transom and its safety chain inadequate. But none of that mattered in my family. If it happened on your watch, mitigating circumstances weren't even a courtesy. As I rowed back to the dock, an invoice for a replacement was already being sought.

"The sunken sedan ought to be motoring out of the lake at any time," Patty murmured.

Patty and I were close to Peanut Hill, when I noticed my mother's older sister, Pat, running up the stairs to my grandparents' cottage. Aunt Pat was known for her pyorrhea, eight children, and constant suffering. When she smiled, it was slow, like a wave cresting on the beach, from one corner to the next, removing itself the same way. Aunt Pat wore a leather belt around her neck as a punctuation point to everything she said. It looked as if it could snap and curl and dance snug to your rear end if my aunt felt you were too cheeky. The belt was hand-tooled, I think she said, by relatives of Wild Bill Cody himself. He and my grandfather, her father, had apparently ridden the ranges of Nebraska or Colorado. Or maybe it was Wyoming—I could never keep the details straight. I was always focused on the whereabouts of the belt.

I visited my Aunt Pat one summer when I was a preteen and watched as she peeled ten pounds of potatoes every afternoon for the evening meal. I helped her fold clothes and vacuum the main floor. I made out with one of her sons, an older cousin, in a closet full of old winter jackets, and never went to confession. After he fled from a Catholic seminary five years later we never spoke again. Their dysfunction was different than ours. It was alluring.

Apparently at the moment I saw Aunt Pat running up the stairs she was responding to a weather report repeated by her youngest son who was most likely reading comics by the old black Emerson radio on Mup's porch. There was a tornado watch in Saint Cloud, he screamed down to the shore. Not much time, the women knew from experience. Entire cottages were known to have blown away between the first whiff of a storm and its last breath.

While Patty was trying to see if she could recognize any of the boys on the public beach, I began to realize that my mother's attempts to wave us back to shore were taking on an urgency as her bandeau slipped a little, revealing a swathe of white breast, as if a beacon, guiding us home. Patty wasn't amused, assuming it one more attempt by our mother to interfere with our meeting the townies—until she noticed the green-tinged sky at the very border of the horizon, the stillness of the lake, and beginning of the stench of fish knowing they were about to die. And then, suddenly came the roar, like an earthquake, or a tidal wave.

No words passed between us as we pulled on the oars. Our thighs rubbed each other, giving solace, while the lake debris flung past—beach rafts, skis, inner tubes, sandals, a life jacket, plastic toys, oars, and fishing rods. *This is what roily water means*, I remember thinking, water black with anger, swirling, oily. The polka dots on Patty's suit turned to ellipses, and she began swearing, giving us a cadence to which we could automatically pull the boat forward. I focused on the oar locks wiggling from their screws with each pull and the worms left over from a fishing trip the week before floating from their red coffee can of soil. The container had Folgers printed on it in large white letters—Mountain Grown. When Juan Valdez and his donkey came later, I pictured his sombrero taking flight.

"Go, goer, goes, o'er, sole, roe," I began.

Patty told me to shut up.

When we reached shallow water, we beached the boat and stumbled along the rocky shore to find our mother. Her French twist was unraveled, the dock was breaking apart, and fish already bobbed on the surface, dead with the beginning of bloat, their color a pall of gray.

"That happened fast," I screamed at Patty.

"What?" she yelled. "What did you say?"

"So many fish. They're dead. Look!"

"They're just fish, you moron! Let's go!" she shouted, grabbing my arm.

The smell was overpowering. It was as if the lake were retching, spewing the contents of the floor to the surface.

The first room upon entering the backdoor of our cottage was the kitchen. A splintery door held shut with a latch was immediately to the left of the entry in a recessed alcove. The door, rarely opened, led to a damp cellar, complete with a dirt floor and mold covered walls. The steps were open, raw wood, no banister. A ledge ran along the steps, a cutout in the cement where my mother stored jars of jelly or fruit that she and my grandmother canned over the course of the summer in the event of a nuclear attack. We never ate them, not so much for the lack of war, but because my mother was afraid of bacteria. There were years of jars encased in spider webs, the lids filthy with the dirt and debris of animals, and from the settling of the cottage.

We trailed each other down the stairs, touching the damp cement walls with our fingertips, trying to stay balanced. My eleven cousins and younger sister were huddled around my grandmother who had lit a votive candle and was leading them in the recitation of the rosary—fifty-three Hail Mary's, six Our Father's, six Glory Be's, and the Apostles Creed. Grandma never went anywhere without her string of fifty-nine blessed beads unless an occasion required something a bit more discrete. In that case she would employ her mini-beads, a set of ten pieces of round glass. The "minis" allowed grandma to pray in a finger jingling rhythm, within the confines of her pocket, moving five times around, unless she lost count. She looked like she had Parkinsons. (When the "auto-rosary" was marketed years after her death, I imagined how grandma would have loved strapping a set of beads to the steering wheel of her Chevy.)

The rosary was a complicated set of prayers with special introductions called mysteries. There were five Joyful Mysteries, five Sorrowful, and five Glorious. Each mystery was prescribed for certain weekdays. On this particular day, a Thursday, the Joyful Mysteries were said. The same would have held if it had been a Monday—Joyful. Before each group of ten Hail Mary's, Grandma made the mystery announcement. "The first mystery is the Annunciation," said Grandma.

A mystery indeed. The Virgin Mary impregnated by the Holy Spirit. The Virgin Birth. The beginning of the delusion for prospective nuns. The allusion of happiness. Believe. Grandma glared at Patty and me. She could feel the bumping of our brains. She had heard this discussion before.

An entire rosary could take upwards of an hour and we were on the fifth Joyful Mystery—Finding Jesus in the Temple, when we noticed the wind had stopped. My younger cousins had ceased their thumb sucking by this time and were staring trance-like at Grandma's bony fingers walking along her beads. An entire rosary was hypnotic. For a while after my mother died, its strict cadence kept away intrusive thoughts. I think Grandma knew its power. For good luck, she continued praying ten more Hail Marys as we emerged from the cellar.

On the lake everything had changed. The storm had wrapped its arms around each curve, a possessive lover bent on satiation. Huge boulders had washed to shore, and boats, docks, and rafts were beached on the sandbar. We knew the lake pits had been rearranged and that we could no longer trust our quadrants. The fish would move to new holes and fishermen would have to wander around the lake in their pursuit. Later I saw that the Blessed Virgin on the convent beach had lost her outstretched hands. The Benedictines were seen for weeks sifting the sand with strainers looking for them.

I kept an eye on the shoreline for anything familiar—Patty's graduation Bulova, sunglasses and bathing caps, anything sky blue, sun hats, towels, pieces of the Evinrude—as if I were looking for evidence of gods, spirits, demons.

Was it an omen, this violent retching of the lake? After all, it was only four months later that my mother stained the carpet by the side of her bed, the night she died, leaving behind that rusty red blotch.

It was during that final summer season that my caution gave way to spontaneity, and I managed to convince my mother I was ready to swim across the lake—about a mile and a half from our dock to the public beach. My sense of adventure just happened to coincide with my father's return to Chicago, thus eliminating the risk of failure in his presence, and of course, the subsequent story which would detail any mistakes.

My mother was agreeable under the condition that Patty row beside me with instructions to toss a life jacket at a moment's notice, something I knew needed to be coordinated between her attention to any males in the area and my flailing body. The swim was a rite of passage, something that most cousins attempted at some point during late adolescence, to separate them from the "little kids". It brought a certain privileged status among the lake dwellers, not the least of which was being able to swim outside of the life rope which bobbed between the two cottages like a playpen.

As I prepared, my mother's head rested on the back of a metal beach chair with her eyes closed, flecks of rust swirling around the black stubby hairs on her legs. I thought later, after she died, that her lack of attention to my preparation indicated that she must have had confidence in me, that I would succeed. Besides, I convinced myself, she might have sensed embarrassment at being fussed over even though potential harm lay ahead in the numerous drop-offs, snapping turtles, and seaweed. And even though at the time I wasn't conscious of the swim as a test of my mettle, I would remember it as a practice run sans mother. Perhaps she intuited this rationale as well, thus explaining her insouciance.

She was wearing a one-piece bathing suit that day, with an attached pleated skirt that had stretched to an A-line over the course of two or three summers. The top of the bodice had a wire insert—"support" my mother called it—and the net effect was one of separate domiciles. She refused to replace the suit until she lost a few pounds; the result was one angry welt circling the top of each thigh. I suspected the constant sting around her panty line served as a reminder as she counted calories and eliminated the maraschinos from her Perfect Manhattans.

All the adult females dressed for the lake in a similar manner—pleats and polka dots, sophisticated plaids and stripes, the warp and weft of fabric in a state of constant strain. The men wore baggy trunks over their slim torsos with the exception of one uncle who wore something bright and form fitted. He always stood a little too close to where others were sitting, or positioned himself alone, on the dock, in profile. At least that's how it seemed.

"What is it, Patty," I would complain, "that makes it impossible not to stare?"

And then we would hold hands and jump feet first into the water, releasing bubbles as we giggled back to the surface. The male body was alien to us, absurd, showy. When we heard about the concept of Penis Envy, we were confused.

"How in the world would one cope with something like that?" Patty groaned. And then we would go back to rifling through *National Geographic* in Grandma's cottage.

Patty was in our aluminum fishing boat busy coating her body with Johnson's Baby Oil to which she had added a few drops of iodine. Her two-piece suit was a mesmerizing sea of polka dots, some more strategically placed than others. She was regaling the audience on the dock with stories of her successful swim two years before, how she began with the perfect breaststroke which imperceptibly melted into a pastiche of backstroke and crawl stroke, broken only with respites of water treading. The finale, Patty demonstrated to whomever was listening, was the butterfly.

"And then I went underwater for a moment and did a perfect headstand. The townies actually were clapping when I came up for air. I have to admit, I held my breath longer that time than any other I can remember."

Our two cottages were filled to capacity that weekend with both of my mother's sisters and their children. Most of the guests had already made their way down the steps to the lake for the afternoon, even ungainly old "MG," who dropped into a beach chair as I dove, my mind chanting:

"Ah, Granny Gross, Granny Gross. What a huge derriere you have."

Slimy boulders became dislodged as my body skimmed over their surface, and when my suit snagged on their jagged outcroppings, I knew I had gone too deep, my first mistake. Reflexively, I ran both hands over my arms and legs checking for bloodsuckers and made my way to the surface wondering if I had enough air. Patty was standing in the boat, hands cupped over her eyes, rocking dangerously as she pivoted from side to side, trying to locate me.

"Leeches!" I sputtered to her when my head crashed through the surface, my heart threatening explosion. And though I wasn't even fifty yards from the adult assemblage, I managed a wobbly smile and wave, showing my spunk, and humor. I doubt anyone noticed. Patty threw her oars into the water and exited as I thrashed around trying to gain some composure. I understood her departure. It had taken only a brief afternoon of rock hunting one summer to discover the lake was rife with leeches.

(We had been drifting for hours that day inside a huge black inner tube, our feet dragging along the bottom of the lake disturbing rocks and their inhabitants. By the time we stood, our appendages were plastered with the fat rolling things and then speckled with red dots after we rubbed each other with sand to remove them. Madeleine had enjoyed the episode. She always thought we were too snotty for our own good.)

My eyes were always wide open when I swam, even before the leech episode. Primarily I wanted to avoid encountering dead fish that bobbed atop the water. There was nothing more unnerving than to execute a tidy dive off the end of the dock only to end up in a face-off with the opaque eyes of a dead crappie. But the overriding reason for my visual diligence was to avoid the lake pits where the gods might be lying in wait. My imagination swept over the miles of terrain of the lake bottom, the valleys and rises, the meadows and seaweed forests inhabited with these invisible gods. I knew only too well that I had probably offended their sensibilities, particularly with this attempt at showmanship. Certainly Patty had.

Fish darted out of the way as I cut through the seaweed, pulling at the water with my hands. Inch by inch I clawed and yanked and opened a path for my body. Moving my head back and forth like a pendulum, I grabbed a breath before rotating through the water to expel it on the other side while my feet made gentle slaps on the surface. Initially my body forged a fairly straight swath, and I entertained myself imagining I was swimming across the English Channel. I cupped the water, reaching with long strokes, diligently in sync with my head, my legs and feet, until I could stand the suspense no longer and allowed myself the first flip of the day to view the distant shoreline and my relatives. It was an unfortunate calculation on my part. I was barely out of the gate. I could see Madeleine cupping her hand around her cigarette, the glint of her Zippo, the flick of the tobacco off her tongue. I could tell by the direction of her turned head that she had become interested.

The next time I lifted my eye to the horizon I could see dust billowing on the dirt road which wound itself around the lake separating cottages from farmland. As my body glided through the water, I recalled slipping under the barbed wire fence into the pasture behind our cottage to smoke hollow reeds of grass. Patty and I would often do this together, holding the slender stalks like the models we saw in magazines, exclaiming "Dahling, careful now of those cow muffins!"

Patty and I understood the topography of storms, especially the ones that blew across the farm region, gaining momentum when they hit the lake. Sometimes the air would be so thick with humidity, so still, that the very sound of thunder made you tip your head back, smile, and take a deep breath. And when the rain came, it was like a breaking fever. Lake storms mimicked the ones in our own lives, the way they could build from a whiff of a disagreement to sudden fury, then recede as quickly as they came, leaving a wake of damage. They reminded us of our father who could lacerate egos with words. And the nuns who vented their tempests with well-placed slaps, noisy in their execution. Or sweet Sister Lavina, escorted from a spelling bee one morning for throwing holy water over the heads of the contestants while muttering, "Blessed are the poor in spirit, the meek, mourners, and merciful non-fornicators."

Patty and I knew there had to be prodromal signs before these breakdowns in behavior, and weather—signs that we needed to figure out. We understood there was no such thing as a benign calmness.

Every summer we would escape into a farmhouse abandoned after one such violent storm, passing outbuildings and roofs scattered throughout the fields of immature and deformed corn. The kitchen stood at the back of the farmhouse, accessing an outdoor cellar and garden. The garden was wildly overgrown and garish, its beauty mocking the destruction that lay immediately inside the backdoor. The cupboards were ripped from the walls, leaving lath and plaster to spill over them like flour. The appliances were overturned and dented as if they had taken repeated blows. One chair stood upright by a window where a cherry tree grew into the house, dropping fruit year after year onto the linoleum. Someone had covered the walls with modern pictographs, obscenities that focused on women. The anonymous hostility left us shaken.

There were two bedrooms upstairs with built-in dressers sitting in little nooks draped with broken glass from mirrors. In one, an irregular outline of a rug was etched into the pine floor. Part of the floor was burned, charred from a fire that was set in the corner of the room. Patty hoped it was the heat from lovers. The floors were warped and stained from rotted food, animal droppings, cigarette burns, and something oily. A mattress was slapped into a corner, exposing the dull stigma of fertility, and without touching it, we would walk right to its side and bend close to stare at the layers of secrets harbored on its surface as surely as if there were two bodies squirming there at that very moment.

We imagined...

The mother of this farm family as morose and moody, self-involved (Patty and I hadn't heard of narcissism yet,) a woman with long, wiry black hair, which grew thick and wild in the muggy air of summer. (So did ours, curls so tight we would forego combing some days when the air hung wet and sour.) Her eyes were tinted a ridiculous blue, tiny and lashless, just spots of color without any adornment, not even much of an iris. And she was tall, like the angular line of poplars surrounding the fields.

We saw her as alone but not lonely. Illusive. In fact it was as if she were a shell containing secrets rather than organs, nothing more, always looking for her reflection in windows, mirrors, and the glassiness of the lake, needing constant verification that she was, in fact, alive. (And indestructible? Was this the lesson to be learned from our tale as it matured with us, until the final chapter?)

Patty hypothesized that she likely married in a civil ceremony in St. Paul one hot summer evening, wearing a tight white suit with a short peplum jacket that was beaded on the bosom with roses, stems and all, a few thorns protruding. (I think at some point we drew pictures of this wedding outfit, so enamored were we by her small waist.) While this could have been the result of an adventurous attack of artiness by her seamstress, the Justice of the Peace and witnesses saw it as a statement about her maternal instinct. They gossiped, I told Patty, especially about the thorns protruding from her breasts. (Most likely this wardrobe anomaly was our mental image of Roman Catholic lingerie—chastity belts and barbed wire.) The narrow, straight skirt was slightly below her knee, a perfect length for her seamed stockings and spiked heel. A jaunty pillbox hat was hooked to one side of her upswept hair. A veil was starched upward, not necessarily as an invitation to a kiss, but rather to furnish an unobstructed view of the proceedings. Clearly she didn't believe in fairytales.

Her children were cast into her shadow, and although never the object of her scorn (but perhaps deceit), they felt that they were not very desirable; that mother love (which came from God, according to Sister Mary Agatha, one of our barren teachers) had some qualifications to which they weren't privy. She begrudgingly cared for them, combing two heads of thick hair, feeding them, finding them clothing. And they loved her, of course (again as stipulated by Sister Mary Agatha as messenger from God), yet suffered from anxiety in her presence. She always seemed remote, and what kept her physically located on their farmland was elusive even to her daughters.

She often walked the shoreline by the lake, detached from her surroundings, immersed in music that no one else could hear. Her daughters followed her at a distance, trailing after their frayed umbilicus with a sense of impending doom. And even though she glanced with half-slit eyes over her shoulder at frequent intervals, it appeared she was in the throes of her own tumult, drowning the pleas of her children.

And then it happened: She failed to return from the water's edge. The crops immediately began to wither in the cool morning breeze. Oddly, the girls were strengthened for a moment and, unlocking their arms from each other, they upended the house searching for her secrets. They broke the windows so they would hear her silent footfalls in the night. They walked the shore of the lake and searched for her between rows of corn until dusk when a sickle-shaped moon forged a narrow path through the woods. Sometimes they would suddenly find themselves prostrate, pressing their faces into a furrow as if it were her breast, caressing the soil and inhaling her odor. Laying their ears gently on the ground, they heard her swiftly retreating footsteps never stopping even at the lake's edge. It was there they pleaded for her to take them back to her womb. "Let us fill you!" they yelled together, to the wind and the stars, the earth and water.

Like most children, Patty and I were both repelled and intrigued by the worst possible fate of childhood—mother-death. The thought was intoxicating in its impossibility, and in that sense we were drawn to the story, flirted with it, imagined the worst only because we knew we would be spared.

"If you say things out loud, they will never happen," I always told Patty. (How did I know my magical thinking wouldn't protect my mother?) And so we continued summer after summer to be drawn to the abandoned farmhouse and the story of loss until Patty found the perfect epitaph to let our tale rest in peace.

Epitaph
Heap not on this mound
Roses that she loved so well;
Why bewilder her with roses,
That she cannot see or smell?
She is happy where she lies
With the dust upon her eyes.

"Change the dust to water," I said after the recitation. "The mother went into the lake."

"The poem is from Edna St. Vincent Millay, you klutz," Patty sniffed. "We're changing nothing. It stays this way."

Patty had stopped rowing and was floating in the distance, waiting for me to catch up to the boat. The unusually frigid water signaled Peanut Hill, a reminder that natural springs, which fed the lakebed, also fed the lake pits. We were more than halfway across, and I was exhausted, spending a great deal of time on my back, my blood idling, tracing the shoreline with my eyes shut. I turned a bit on my side and curled into myself as if I was in a womb. I wished we were sitting on top of Peanut Hill right now, lying on the faded blue-and-white checkered tablecloth, whispering stories from our buzzing brains.

"I think I can still see Madeleine's cigarette from here," Patty taunted.

I always had dreams of quicksand, of being swallowed slowly in black, fetid muck. At the instant when only my long blonde ponytail was visible laying on the water's surface would someone tow me out. My rescuer was always unremarkable; the details of his countenance eluded me. Maybe I wanted to drown.

This dream flooded my senses at the moment my big toe lightly brushed the bottom of the Lake, closer to shore than I imagined. I rested.

Unwittingly…

That's the word that floats through my mind. Unwittingly I am walking across a field into a forest that has a path, a well-worn path with trees forming a lush canopy on either side. The colors and shapes of the trees are dramatic. I can never describe the intensity of feeling I have for that path—it is unabashed love, first love, romantic and sensual. I am feeling safe because I have not been the first to pass this way; others have walked before me. There are no enchanted mushrooms glinting in the sun, no ruby red apples, slippers, or pumpkin coaches to distract me. I feel as though I have known this place all of my life and that at any moment I will see members of my family reaching out to take my hand. When my foot hits the very edge of the quicksand, I am stunned, too stunned to leap back. My weight immediately submerges one of my legs to the knee. Quicksand. Its danger is concealed beneath a veneer of normalcy. And then I think of mother's milk.

"You can stand now!" Patty screamed, embarrassed that for some reason I was thrashing around in a sudden panic.

There were a few families on the public beach, enjoying the fading afternoon sun. I think some were watching me, and others, Patty, standing in the boat coaxing me to get out of the water. I felt as if I had been burped from the bottom of the lake, turned inside out, my leg muscles languid and worthless. My accomplishment was tempered with a sense of foreboding, like the prologue to a new fairytale. I had no desire to move until I saw our red and white Chris Craft speedboat, one of my cousins at the wheel. It seemed to be listing dramatically to one side—or maybe I was, and just as my spirits lifted with what I envisioned as my mother, I noticed the familiar glow, a speck of fire, from the tip of MG's Pall Mall filled the frame.

"You made it, sis," she growled with her late afternoon fetid breath. "I'll be damned. Climb in."

Abandonment was nothing new in fairytales, and afterwards, I would try to retell this story of our own creation casting the mother as the punitive step-mom. I wanted to be angry with her. But that never quite rang true. Somehow the story lost its authenticity.

I always saw this mother as having her own life course even though it seemed to conflict with my notion of the mother-role. And her emptiness? I keep wondering how that happened. I wanted the girls to fill her up, to be enough. But I knew that wasn't possible. You have to fill your own soul.

Until my mother died, I always felt relief that the girls never found the secrets. I wanted this woman to disappear and leave them with their mother-death story, as dissatisfying as it was. When she vanished into the lake, I felt some solace. Knowing her inner life would have been too much, too devastating. Even fairy tales shouldn't require that amount of anguish. Over the years, my intimacy with my own secret changed everything. There was nothing lonelier. And I wonder if this is why my mother remains illusory. She vanished with her secrets too.

My family was very cavalier around the topic of death as if those who died were careless and came from poor breeding. We were too pretty, too smart, too effervescent, to be removed from the earth. The only death that I really remembered as a child had been that of Mrs. Bartholomew, our one-eyed baby-sitter who sometimes sat for my sisters and me when my parents left town for a weekend. It took us a while to get used to Mrs. Bartholomew. First of all, she wasn't symmetrical with only one faded blue eye balanced by a cotton ball in the other socket. And as if that weren't distressing enough, Mrs. Bartholomew suffered from a nervous twitching around the cotton squatter that threatened to dislodge it.

When she died, my mother took Patty and me to her wake. It was the first time we had seen a dead body, and from what we could tell, it was an opportunity for the family to have a free-for-all with makeup and clothing. Mrs. Bartholomew was a simple woman who lived in housecoats and cold cream. Until she died. Then she was swabbed with a line of lipstick which stretched ear to ear, injected with hair bouffant, and relieved of the cotton ball. After nearly falling into the casket trying to see Mrs. B's socket, Patty and I decided Mrs. Bartholomew, without her cotton ball, was better than imagining what the hole looked like for all those years.

And then it happened: our own mother failed to return to us one brutally cold Sunday morning. We were grossly unprepared, too, even though Patty and I had spent endless hours crafting our story of mother-death, flagrantly courting this calamity, summer after summer, all the while smug and confident that our mother would never vanish. Yet she did, like the farm woman of our imagination. It seemed God's Will had become the ultimate childhood betrayal.

Chapter 7
The Funeral

If you asked me even now when my mother died, I might say, January nineteenth or maybe the twentieth—something within that general timeframe; I can't be sure without rummaging through my white scrapbook from grade school. When my mother gave it to me for my tenth birthday, she said the cover was "leatherette." Three years later, in 1963, most of the letters spelling "memories" etched in raised gold paint on its cover had peeled away, leaving only a faint scarring of *'em'* and *'es,'* looking more like the word "emesis" than anything else. That's where I kept my mother's obituary pasted on its own page right after some old certificates signed by Sister Delphine for completing the Preparatory Course in Piano as prescribed by the Precollegiate Department of Alverno College in Milwaukee. It was the piano curriculum of choice at Saint Michael's Catholic School.

My inability to remember was selective in that I could clearly recall everything about Sister Delphine. Perhaps this was because she was a dream of a piano teacher, sleeping through most lessons and only awakened by complete silence. I ran up and down scales to the metronome of her snorts and chortles, improvising with grace notes when I felt brave. Sister Delphine's sleepiness was the direct result of an increase in her seizure medication after she crumpled unceremoniously to the floor during one of my lessons. Sister Cecil

Gabriel, who counseled me after the incident, explained that in the event of another attack, I should "gently slide a pencil between her teeth and try not to get bitten."

When it happened the first time, I imagined I had somehow killed Sister Delphine by my miserable and angry scales, until I found myself distracted by her wimple which skittered across the wood floor, freeing a cap of gray split ends. Assuming that all nuns were bald and featureless underneath their habits, I regarded this a monumental moment of good fortune for my popularity. In a repressed environment such as Saint Michael's, Sister Delphine's split ends were sexy.

After her seizure, I attempted to memorize most of my pieces so that I could keep an eye on Sister. We managed to make it through the intermediate level with only two other incidents. By that time, I was carrying discarded Popsicle sticks along with my weekly music in a brown vinyl music pouch, one glued to the other for quick access.

For a while, my mother's obituary occupied a page with an autographed postcard featuring Bobby Darin that Gramps had sent me from Las Vegas. It was signed, "Mickey, From Bobby Darin" from "The Fabulous Flamingo." They shared a page in my leatherette scrapbook for utilitarian purposes only—two events in the same year, one before the other: mother dies followed by Bobby Darin. Besides, the page had space. I didn't like Bobby Darin's songs all that much either, especially after I received a warning from Mrs. Morris, the principal of Saint Michael's, for bringing the postcard to school.

"His lyrics are offensive, my dear," she admonished me. "He doesn't make any attempt in 'Splish Splash I Was Taking a Bath' to get his clothes on. His words might create impure thoughts."

I remember Mrs. Morris handing me my keepsake with the tips of her fingers, as if she were being unchaste. And her lips. I can picture them perfectly. They were pursed.

At first my memory was exhausting if it wasn't about *her*. The week that my mother was buried, Harpo Marx broke his silence. He said he was leaving show business. I wondered if he had discussed it with any of his brothers beforehand, especially Groucho.

("Say the secret word, Harpo, and win a hundred dollars.")

("Quit," Harpo barked.)

The Nash Rambler won top honors for car of the year. The January 23rd *Wheaton Daily Journal* reported the temperature would plunge to twenty below zero by 8:30 a.m., heralding my mother's frigid funeral at 10:00 a.m. Gerald Covelli, a Chicagoland gangster was transferred from a Wheaton jail into the witness protection program, and mentally challenged children were called "retarted." But that wasn't unusual—that I would notice a spelling error in the paper. I had a cigar box painted black with a gold *M* on the lid containing scores of holy cards won for my spelling prowess.

"Your word, young lady, is *olivaceous*," said Sister Lavinia pointing her simple white wimple in my direction.

I may have curtsied unintentionally while I dealt with my internal chaos.

(*Ah, but I know all about olives*, I thought, brushing a little tobacco from the face of Saint Bernard, Patron Saint of Beekeepers. I wondered if Sister meant the Spanish Queen stuffed with Stilton cheese. Or the small pimentoed variety for a dry martini. Oh! My parents loved Buckeyes! That's a martini made with a black olive. They even use the juice from the olives and called their drinks dirty. Sorry, Sister!)

"Olivaceous. O-L-I-..."

Later in the month, the *Wheaton Daily Journal* reported that Nancy Whaples had competed for the Miss Illinois County Fair, and Robert Frost had died. So did Joseph Schmitz, Wheaton's last blacksmith.

Plates of ham and pickles, different types of bread, and Entenmann's Crumb Coffee Cake arrived within hours of my mother's death and were spread across every surface of our kitchen. A trail of crumbs grew thick with sorrow as mourners stacked their plates with starch and ate through the interior of the house, moving as if on a conveyor belt that rhythmically carried them by the stunned family members towards the front door and back into the winter afternoon. We were an uncomfortable reminder of the precariousness of life.

"God does not give you any burden that you cannot bear," said Sister Ligouri.

(If that was true, why did people go insane? Or kill themselves? Or drink too much, become addicts, eat their way through packages of chips and cookies?)

While not overdone, at least not at first, it seemed our own grief took the form of eating—roasts, rolls, and relish plates. All of that chewing left little room for conversation, not that anyone tried. Patty and I never spoke of our mother after that morning, except to reiterate the cause of her death whenever we were asked.

"It was a cerebral hemorrhage."

Gasp!

"She was only thirty-six." (Or was it thirty-seven?)

My god.

"Suddenly."

This celebrity was painful.

For the longest while, decades really, I was physically unable to speak about my mother in complete sentences without my teeth chattering uncontrollably, as if the secret threatened me with a seizure if I dared to dislodge it from myself. Just the mechanics of talking about her left me with a clenched jaw, weary and shaken. It was easier (and safer) to remain mostly silent right at first, which I did, until we were left alone, all the relatives gone and casseroles eaten.

Nobody danced at my mother's wake. Nobody said that she was in a better place, that they knew how we felt, that it was for the best. There were no jokes or stories or accolades. Toasts to her life were left undone. Her send-off was held in surreal silence in an austere chapel at Kampp and Sons Funeral Home where we were guided to her by a large black sign sitting on a tripod right inside the entrance. Plastic arrows pointed towards her body. (That way, keep going, you're warm, almost there, just a little further.) *Dorothy Jean Don-*

nelly, it read, in white removable letters, followed with the exact date of her death. (Remember, dammit!)

As I slipped around the corner into the solemn chamber, it seemed I was confronted with miles of wood, polished slippery wood, which only ended when you reached the casket. The task of walking to her seemed unmanageable.

She   was   so   far   away.

Gripping the curve of the pews, I stared straight ahead, pulling myself forward, hand over hand, struggling to reach her before she was sacrificed to the gods. My unblinking, immovable body stared at her for hours that evening, until her chest began a rhythmic breathing. I saw the buttons on her dress move, up, down, up, down. I was elated! There had been a mistake. It happened all the time in dreams. And then Patty sidled next to me somewhere in my reverie with a hiss to move away, that it seemed I was trying to garner sympathy. *More than my share.* I looked away for just a minute, but in that time, I knew my mother was indeed dead.

On the second day of the wake, I sat in an anteroom as relatives and friends visited the chapel, signed the guest book, stayed for a rosary led by Father Lynch, hugged each of us, clutched tissues, and muttered, "I don't know what to say." And "If you need anything." And "I wish there were something I could do." And "You poor girls."

John, my mother's hair stylist, had been called to wash and set her hair at the funeral home. And he did, carefully tending to her wisps so that they looked as though they had escaped naturally from the tight French twist. He clipped a bow to her bang, sweeping it across her brow the way she liked, and selected a lipstick to match her most recent rinse. The latter created a brief buzz around the casket. "Dorothy doesn't look like herself," someone whispered. "Her lips are too plump, or maybe it's the color."

The funeral director was notified to make the needed adjustments to the hue and intensity of the pink dye infusing the formaldehyde that replaced her blood. He toned down her lipstick, as well as her lips. He called John to request a new nail polish. He reshaped her face a bit, you could tell, the next morning she didn't look quite so dead. At least that's what one of the guests said on the final day of the two-day wake.

On the third day was the funeral which my eighth-grade class took time from math to attend. Father Lynch wore white as a symbol of joy to celebrate my mother's entrance into heaven. (Had he received a sign?) It would have been baffling, if it wasn't so ridiculous, that we were to rejoice instead of mourn, and even his voice shook as he looked at Patty and me in the front pew and mentioned *suddenly at thirty-seven leaving three girls*. (Later I would perseverate over the mother from our summer yarn, the one who walked into the lake and *left* her girls behind. The word seemed so purposeful.)

A black limousine sat behind the hearse in front of the church, and as her body slipped out of view except for the hump of the casket, we processed to the cemetery. I stared out the tinted window into the frozen day and wondered why the world hadn't stopped its activity. There wasn't a more cataclysmic event, yet the streets of Wheaton seemed full of life. Normal. A line queued outside the Popcorn Shop. A train whistle broke through our silence. There were some bells tolling farther away. (Was it for her, this death knell?) I imagined the pond was glistening in its usual brilliance as the early afternoon sun peaked, and I closed my eyes envisioning my mother driving away from the park for the last time—but not before I had turned and waved.

> *The casket hangs suspended over the black hole. How far down is six feet, I wonder? Patty weeps into Aunt Shirley's mink coat. Father Lynch clasps my father in a bear hug. He looks uncomfortable. My father does. The prayer for the dead has begun.*

> *God, our Father,*
> *Your power brings us to birth,*

Your providence guides our lives,
And by Your command we return to dust.
Lord, those who die still live in Your presence,
Their lives change but do not end.
I pray in hope for my family
Relatives and friends,
And for all the dead known to you alone.

I allow myself to drift away from this prayer and concentrate on the cold seeping through my leather shoes, numbing my toes, until the final amen.

Aunt Nancy, my father's sister, accosts me as I turn towards the waiting limo. She demands a tear. "You will feel better if you cry," she says, her warm breath grown rancid.

I shrug her off and climb into the backseat, folding myself into the corner nearest the site where the gravediggers have begun moving forward from the shadows. Aunt Nancy blocks my view, leaning into the car. "You can't go on without crying. Let it out."

I close my eyes and concentrate on keeping my breath even. The secret bubbles into my throat like vomit.

"I don't feel well," I whisper to my aunt.

"Just cry," she says again.

On the fourth day I went to school. My eighth-grade teacher never mentioned the event which kept me from three days of homework.

After the funeral food ran its course, Annelle Peterson from Wheaton College was hired to prepare dinner, iron, and keep an eye on our post-school activities. However, she refused to perform the most essential task of running the evening household—she would neither mix, stir, nor pour my father's beloved elixir, his Perfect Manhattan. In fact, Annelle wouldn't touch the sweaty pitcher no matter how loud or long my father tinkled the ice cubes in his glass from his perch in the living room. I admired her courage, but then she had Billy Graham in her corner while my sisters and I had a silent Christ Almighty. Annelle cried the day she left and slipped a few of her homespun recipes into my hand. My father told us he had never been comfortable with Annelle anyway.

"I felt like she was staring at me, passing judgment," he said. "She was a fanatic. Too uptight. Who needs it. You girls can make my Manhattans."

By April, a black granite monument appeared at the head of my mother's grave. It looked like the death was permanent. Her name was chiseled in a contemporary manuscript, ***Dorothy Jean 1925-1963*** as was my father's, although the hyphen between his date of birth and death was like a long-held note pitched between here and there. The gravesite looked like a permanent crime scene—the black dirt retaining its fresh appearance in the snow, like a chalk outline. With the ground thawed, my father was able to plant a small evergreen on each side of the stone. He even laid his own weed-free sod, although the groundskeeper assured him there was a greenhouse of Kentucky Bluegrass on the premises.

After that first winter, my mother never went without a grave blanket, a woven mass of pine boughs and ribbon extending the full length of the plot. Most graves had blankets in the winter at Saint Michael's Cemetery. Some were decorated with pinecones and berries, and others had a contemporary feel, maybe a little raffia and wheat with a plaid bow. My father always opted for the all-natural grave blanket, simple and thick with greenery.

It only took a few months before my mother's closet was filled with my father's summer suits, her clothes distributed to relatives, the leftovers to charity. The only remembrances of her existence within their bedroom were a Prince Machiabelli flacon, a cracked Saint Jude statue, and a faded red stain by her side of the bed. For a few months, the card table that my parents used for their bridge group was stacked with engraved stationary, holy cards, envelopes, a roll of nickel stamps, and sheets of addresses. It sat in the middle of the living room like an altar. Mups organized this detail, thanking everyone for his or her attention during our time of need. It was all done according to Emily Post, within the allotted time frame, with the correct paper and writing utensil.

"Within the month!" she admonished us. "Preferably before Valentine's Day!"

She made certain that my sisters and I each had one of the holy cards distributed at my mother's funeral. The cards were intended to honor the saint who somehow exemplified the deceased life. The Blessed Virgin dressed in a pale blue flowing robe, pastel lipstick, and touch of blush adorned the front of these particular cards, even though Saint Jude Thaddeus, the Patron Saint of Hopeless Cases, was my mother's favorite. Patty and I both knew our mother had her own holy cards featuring Saint Jude stashed in a bedside table. These cards gave precise instructions on how to garner his attention and persevere despite dire circumstances. Prayers to Saint Jude were filled with words like "hopeless," and "desperate," and "despite."

"Saint Jude Thaddeus," one began.

"I implore you to look upon me with compassion.

Do not despise my poor prayer.

Do not let my trust be confounded.

God has granted you the privilege of aiding mankind in the most desperate of cases.

Oh, come to my aid that I may praise the mercies of God!

All my life I will be your faithful client until I can thank you in heaven.

Amen."

These prayers were novenas, the Cadillac of supplications requiring a certain compulsion, and of course, superstition. Novenas were prescribed prayers to be recited at the same hour followed by three of each: Our Father, Hail Mary, and Glory Be to the Father. They were prayed for nine days in a row. If you missed a day, you went back to the beginning. Period. If you were in a hurry, a novena marathon could be implemented; the nine days would be condensed into one, with a prayer said at precisely the same time for nine hours in a row. I believed attention to the rules was much more important than the actual prayer. Somehow it showed obedience, subservience, and most of all, desperation. You added your supplication somewhere in the prayer, where it said "add your own intention here"— not before or after and never more than once. And then you waited. Most times the answer remained elusive. Saint Jude Thaddeus, like the Lord, answered in "many different ways" said the fine print. One of those ways, it seems in retrospect, was death.

I pictured these prayers written on the leeward side of a million kites with tails of requests making their way to Saint Jude Thaddeus from all over the world.

"I beseech you, implore, beg, appeal."

I soothed myself with the oft-repeated belief that she was safe now. That's what I told myself. I maintained this mantra to make sense of this disaster, to steady myself. "She is safe." And remarkably, as firm as I was in that belief, I cannot remember any substance behind it. Had I internalized some of her secrets that were too frightening to articulate, much less remember? Was there something stalking me, waiting to reveal itself? Something that would explain my fear for my mother? I hesitated to pray to Saint Jude on my own behalf and that of my worm-ridden memory, but for my mother, I prayed my own novena, hoping the Saint would overlook my skepticism.

"Saint Jude Thaddeus," I began. "If you could see to it that my mother is no longer desperate and hopeless, I would appreciate your consideration. I'll try to go to Mass every holy day if you wouldn't mind checking on her once in a while. She may be frightened, or lonely. Thank you.

Amen." (Times nine.)

Besides the picture of the Blessed Virgin and the Hail Mary, the holy cards were printed with my mother's birthday and date of death. I was giving myself a daily quiz by April, a ritual of sorts, peppering my internal mind chatter with questions of fact.

(When *did* your mother die? What was her date of birth?) Calculate. (She was *how* old?) Add, subtract, divide.

Like the Baltimore Catechism, the text for Catholic doctrine, rote memorization was the only way to answer questions of faith. It didn't make any more sense than my mother's death.

"Why did God make you?" asked Sister Mary Catherine.

"Well," I replied. (*Why not?* I thought somewhat defensively.) "We all know that God made me to know Him, to love Him, and to serve Him in this world, but I'm quite unsure of my mother's date of death."

I *couldn't* remember her date of death, and then later, her birthday, what she looked like, or my Christmas presents that year. As luck would have it, all that I remembered were the words, "Please don't hurt me." Words that I kept secret. My mother's words. The last words I heard before she died.

I tried to preserve the contents of the linen closet for a while in the exact order that my mother left them—the sheets and towels newly folded, the stacked soap and arranged cosmetics. I did the same with the kitchen, alphabetizing spices, wiping jar lids, and placing them in a row label side out. I crawled on my hands and knees with a dust rag sprayed with polish, wiping the tile that surrounded the area rug in the living room. I scoured the bottom of the garbage pail, removed fingerprints from the doors, did the laundry on schedule. When I came home from school, I imagined it was my mother's doing, all this sorting and organizing. My grandmother cried when she came for a visit and saw that I had scoured the sink with Ajax, cleaned the crumbs from the toaster, and dusted the top of the fridge.

"Look at the sink!" Mups whispered, grabbing my arm. "It has been shined perfectly." But her compliment only amplified her desolation, and of course my own. I turned away from her grasp and inched my mother's old ceramic cookie jar slightly closer to the Sunbeam Mixmaster where it belonged.

I saved the Christmas stocking that I made for her in Girl Scouts. It was in the shape of an old-fashioned boot with red ribbon for laces. I put it in my scrapbook along with her nurse's cap that she wore only for a short time after she married. I placed a three-quart

Mason jar filled with buttons in my room, buttons that my mother had removed from discarded clothing. Where else was there a concentration of four hundred thirty-three things that held her fingerprints? I felt lucky. My father gave me her cameo ring, a gift from an old boyfriend. And I remembered she had told me a story about him, how she'd awakened from a dead sleep at the very moment he was shot out of the sky during the Korean War. They were engaged, or about to be, or maybe that was my fairytale. I also inherited a sterling silver charm bracelet with thirteen mementoes she received throughout her life. Yet I didn't know the story behind any of those charms, so I made up my own.

What I didn't need to fabricate, though, was *that night*—what I witnessed and what was reported. Those first months I relived the memory over and over and tried to reconcile the diagnoses of my mother's demise. These interpretations competed for more time, more energy, more concentration, which left me with more internal chaos.

"Can't you even add two plus two?" my father asked when I showed him my first term grades from high school. Nine months had passed, already.

"How can someone go from the top of their class to the bottom in less than a year? You're grounded."

My face was unflinching as noise coursed through my body, top to bottom, words riding my blood drowning out his blather—(so what, shut up, simply cut, hut, hut).

"I have already grounded myself!" I wanted to scream, but I couldn't over the noise in my head.

The secret had filled my brain, worming itself into every fold. No wonder I couldn't concentrate. The only thing it didn't control was my breathing. Even swallowing was disjointed. My father got angry with my sighs.

"Is something wrong?" he would glare.

"What?" I would snap back. "Something wrong?"

"All that noise. Quit sighing. And smile, for god's sake."

Before I had time to execute one thought, another had supplanted that one and then the next and the next. My brain was a cobble of prefixes and suffixes, -dis, -non, -un, -ness. I tried to read assignments backwards first. The last paragraph became the anchor. When I reached the beginning, my ability to recall had capsized. I wondered if you could have a cerebral infarct and lose your memory instead of your life.

Incredibly, no one stopped this catastrophe. Sister Claire, my homeroom advisor gave me C's in citizenship. "You're not trying," she said.

It was the smiling thing again. I wasn't making homeroom pleasant. She was right. I was nervous, and agitated, and perhaps a little surly.

"Sister Claire," I wanted to say. "What about this from Ecclesiastes? 'Sorrow is better than laughter: for by sadness of the countenance the heart is made better.'" But I knew Sister Claire really didn't care as much about the contents of my heart as she did about math and Latin.

(Sister! My brain has suddenly taken on the characteristics of a sieve. My mnemonic devices have disengaged from their source. What, dear Sister, beyond ECT might you suggest?)

She never called my father in for a conference but placed me in home economics with a warning to get my zippers straight. My father supplied me with fabric remnants acquired from his job as a textile buyer for Sears. I made skirts without waistbands and shirt-waist dresses with matching sashes and not so straight metal zippers. Once I made a dress out of drapery material. Huge purple flowers peppered every inch of the heavy hopsack cloth—a veritable Monet's garden.

My father didn't seem surprised, really, and seemed pleased with the savings on my wardrobe and perhaps college. All of my available energy was absorbed by the secret, leaving me unable to advocate for myself. Besides, I wasn't thinking about the future, especially my dreams of becoming a pediatrician. I was just surviving.

I tried to jumpstart my concentration by reading my favorite authors. If the book was suspenseful, I read the endings first. I tried to avoid mysteries. Even absurd predicaments, the ones that could never happen, left me shaken. I couldn't suspend my disbelief for a moment. The only stories I managed to read in that genre were from Edgar Allen Poe except for "The Telltale Heart," which caused intense perseveration concerning my own thumping chest. *An American Tragedy* became my favorite book.

I got in the habit of eliminating surprises. Letters, catalogs, newspapers were read back to front. I couldn't go to movies unless someone told me everything would turn out all right. It was the same with television, and stories my sisters told about their day. I always asked first, "Are you okay? Has everything been worked out?" Tell me the last first, the upshot of the whole affair, the final word, cut to the chase. It became my trademark—"She's so upfront, that one." But really I was scared silly.

The afternoon the Fuller Brush Man visited Hawthorne Boulevard, I wasn't in attendance with the other freshmen at Saint Francis High School. I remember this because it was the day after I put Ritz coloring on my hair and broke out in hives. When the doorbell rang, it occurred to me that my mother had another life during the day—a life of salesmen and charities, hairdressers, bridge groups, meal planning, homemaking, much of which I would never know. When I opened the door, he was swiping at the doorknocker with some sort of chemically treated rag looking as if he had just ridden into town on the hose of the latest vacuum. I tried to hide my resentment.

"Hi," he said. "I'm the Fuller Brush Man. I thought I would stop by and see if Dorothy needed anything this week. You're her daughter, aren't you? You look so much like her! Well, at least around the eyes and mouth. Yes, I would swear if I saw you walking down the street I would say, 'That girl reminds me of Dot!' Don't you have school today? Is this a holiday of some sort? Is your mother home?"

His hoses banged against his leg for emphasis. His face was broad and smooth. There was not so much as a mole, whisker, or filled pore to identify him. If I had to pick him from a line-up, I would have to resort to smell. It took me a moment to answer. The Fuller Brush Man was too perfect, too clean and nice and unassuming. That got me the most—the way he assumed all was well with the world.

"You are too damn chirpy!" I wanted to scream.

But that would have been unfair. So I said nothing for a moment, trying to quash the grief. Maybe it was longer than a moment. It was a habit I was developing, brief catatonic lapses into a reverie filled with music, or words in a foreign language of gibberish, sometimes jingles. Distractions to keep me from weeping.

Suddenly, the Fuller Brush Man tilted his pug little nose upward, just slightly. He appeared to be sniffing the air. Was he in search of her perfume? Or maybe he sensed some sort of betrayal of cleansers—that I was sent to the door as a proxy because my mother couldn't face him herself.

"She's not here right now. She's unavailable." I said this forcefully to scare him into not asking the next question. It was I who was terrified, though—afraid that if I spoke the words my teeth would chatter. My body would vibrate. My stomach would heave. It happened almost every time—if I spoke the words aloud.

But I did anyway.

"She died," I said.

His head snapped back. His skin blotched. He sniffed the air some more and began blinking wildly.

"Of what?" he whispered.

"A cerebral hemorrhage," I said so matter of factly. "A cerebral hemorrhage. Suddenly. In January." And then, of course my brain chattered. ("A CVA. A CVA. Happened suddenly on that day. And left a spot of deepest red, by the side of their double bed.")

"We won't be needing any more supplies, I guess. Thanks for coming by."

I stood with him in the open doorway. He stared until the blue of his eyes faded. Drool formed in the corners of his mouth.

"Are you okay?" I asked. Gently at first, and then a little louder. He kept staring, though, and I thought maybe the stain on my soul, the stain from the secret had surfaced. I looked down and he was gone.

He turned back once, at the end of the driveway, looking frightened. I wondered if it was of me, that I might be following him, smelling of death. But I was doubled over by now, clutching my stomach. He held up his hand in a sort of half-wave and seemed to be muttering something, like a prayer. It turned out to be the oath of all Fuller Brush Men.

"I will be courteous; I will be kind; I will be sincere; I will be helpful. I will be courteous; I will be kind; I will be sincere; I will be helpful."

This refrain somehow propelled him down the boulevard. I shut the door.

And so spring-cleaning began.

I've often thought that I should have grabbed the fleshy arm of the Fuller Brush Man that afternoon and escorted him down the hallway, stopping right before the master bedroom door. I'd have left him then, to walk the rest of the way alone while I stood at the threshold stringing together Hail Mary's like a life rope until he reached the site of the stain by the side of the bed. Kneeling by the pinkish hue of the splayed fibers that had been unwound and meticulously scrubbed, the Fuller Brush Man would have touched the area, testing the fibers himself. "I'm afraid the stain is too deep to remove," he might call to me. "Even with Formula 21, 22, or 23..."

But I wouldn't hear him. I would be concentrating too hard on the sound of my mother's satin heel as it careened off her foot that night. I would be squinting in the dark to make out the figure of my father dragging her along the linoleum. My ear would be pressed to the floor by their closed door. She would sound like prey.

Afterwards, the Fuller Brush Man might stop at the room closest to the master, my room. I was certain he would be satisfied with the cleanliness of the shelves, the closet, the dresser. He might be comforted seeing firsthand that the home was being taken care of in the fashion to which it had become accustomed.

(Ah, Fuller Brush Man. These are just the patterns of life, a contest of opposites. Life and death, young and old, night and day, chaos and order. Nothing is fixed except mother and daughter. The apple doesn't fall far from the tree, a pea from her pod, a seedling in sod.)

The brown linoleum in my room was shiny, waxy underneath the braided rug. If the Fuller Brush Man bent down low enough though, he might find a few shards of glass from my clown collection, which I destroyed in its entirety one day in April. It was my first act of voluntary manslaughter. Most of the clowns came from my mother. I suspected they were prompts to get me to smile, to deter my father from further comments about my apparent unhappiness. Instead they filled me with inexplicable shame. My father claimed my moroseness was manipulative, insisting I was after more than my share of attention. But that wasn't true. I just had one of those naturally frowny faces. At least that's what I decided whenever one of my father's fingers stabbed me in the delicate fold between my eyes as he shouted, "Smile!" I always beamed then, you can be sure. I beamed like a sparrow with an open beak. He was my Pavlov.

They were porcelain, bisque, and wood; arms twirled, heads bobbed, bodies rocked; they held dogs, balls, and umbrellas; and I hurled them, one after the other, murderously, to the floor. The last clown that I destroyed was a decanter made of Venetian glass. The stopper head had red lips, a fedora, and black wavy hair poking from the brim. The body was a swirl of primary colors—brilliant reds and blues and yellows. Its smile was garish, too large, too haphazard. Sinister. Maybe that was the point of the gift. Even a few months later, I found minute pieces of that particular clown stuck between the tiles or in the corners of my room. They glinted in the dark, and sometimes I imagined they grew to strobes of flashing light. I would be forced from my bed on those nights to crawl around on the floor while licking the tip of my finger to blot the shards. I would find them on my desk in the morning.

The very day of the broken clowns, I removed the holy card of the Blessed Virgin Mary in the blue robe and outstretched arms from the corner of my mirror. Before I threw her on the heap of glass, I concentrated on my mother's birth date and her date of death. I said them aloud but then promptly forgot them both.

It wasn't long before the pronouncement of the cerebral hemorrhage had grown like a magic bean into a fairy tale of mythic proportions. Without an autopsy, however, this diagnosis was a leap of faith, perhaps a construct, to remove all question of foul play. (Well, she did have headaches, didn't she?) Yet, it became part of my family's oral tradition, and part of the collective lore of the Wheaton community, the Saint Michael's Parish, our school, and neighborhood and friendships. More importantly, the diagnosis of cerebral hemorrhage surrounded my two sisters and me like an endless plague of possibilities as we matured into adults. We tended to every twinge with the diligence of a good mother. Our medical histories were highlighted with one fact—we could be ticking time bombs. It affected birth control choices and life insurance premiums. A headache turned into a migraine; fatigue into dizziness. Aches were because of blood clots coursing unnoticed towards our vulnerable veins. We prayed that our young children wouldn't be motherless. We bargained with God to let us live through birthdays, trips, holidays, milestones. "If you will give me this one trip to Big Fish Lake, just this summer, I won't complain. And by the way, thank you."

Perhaps I should have relented and prayed to Saint Jude Thaddeus, offering him my own desperate case. Instead I continued the destruction of my environment that had begun with the clown decapitation. I broke religious icons representing angels and saints which most Catholic children receive after completing a religious milestone. Rosaries were snapped in two and holy cards were shredded. It was a release from the pressure, if only for a day, that threatened to overwhelm me.

When I learned that cutters mutilated themselves to release their pressure too, freeing their demons, leaving scars behind like translucent lights to follow again and again, I held out the possibility of advancing to the next level, of slicing my wrists wide open, if it became necessary, to protect the secret. Life became easier in those moments, just knowing I could end it.

I studied how to cut, read about it as someone with an eating disorder studied recipes. I imagined well-defined directions legibly scripted on white, very white, parchment taped to the side of the tub.

Directions on Self-Injury:

- *Get rid of any ennui.*
- *Make certain no one is home.*
- *Use a fresh blade; discard the old one through the small slit in the metal container provided; take paper off edge of new blade; if new one is unavailable, clean an old blade of errant debris.*
- *Make transversal and longitudinal cuts (think of the blade as one would the bow of a violin).*
- *Concentrate on a personal timbre.*
- *Float in warm water (imagine a womb).*
- *Let the secret pour out.*

And then I would wonder, wouldn't it be ironic if the secret, that tenacious little thing, remained long after my death and ripened into its own narrative? Without me?

In the end, I traversed my wrist with only one slice. An inch long. Slender.

Unobtrusive. Unsubstantial. Almost a pseudo-slice, a stand-in, a forgery. A serious attempt would have involved more sawing, but I was afraid to submit entirely to the magnitude of my own culpability.

(So, you *could* have stopped the progression of events? The ones that led to her death? You were there? Conscious? You heard? Miss?)

The truth was this—I could have walked into their room when my father walked out.

It was another dark, cold morning when I finally acknowledged my wakefulness, my mother's misadventure, the reason. Strips of headlight poked through my shutters from early morning travelers on the boulevard. I tried to read the spines of my book collection in the dim light but abandoned that distraction, pressing my fingers deep into my eye sockets, distancing myself from my phantasm. I'm used to plagiarizing my dream life by now, making it friendlier, changing outcomes. Usually a futile gesture, I am determined, desperate for relief.

"How could you embarrass me like that? In front of a business partner?" Click. The door to their bedroom closes perfectly with barely an audible sound—key in lock, hand in glove, nail in hole.

"Don't hurt me," my mother whimpers.

I go to their door and open it. I follow her fragrance and squint in the dark until I see her outline on the floor. Her statue of Saint Jude glows.

I yell at my father, as I brush by him. "What's wrong? What's wrong with my mother?"

He is weeping.

My body fits naturally around the curve of her back. I close my eyes and whisper. "It will be okay. Don't worry. I'm here."

Patty stands over me. I feel her warmth. The scene has been interrupted. The debacle derailed. The hole that threatens to swallow my heart stops for a moment. I catch my breath. My mother squeezes my hand. Patty is on her knees. She is praying, clutching our mother's blue rosary. The glass beads cut her hands as the blood from her desperate plea stains the carpet.

I have entered and nothing is as it was. I know this has to be true. Because if not, how will we go on?

"I'll take care of her," he says.

I don't believe him.

And I remain.

But I fail again as the film of that night makes its repeated loop.

My father's words, the ones he said that night after cracking the door just enough for them to bump into my own, foment my desolation.

"Leave her alone," my whisper screams.

"I'll take care of her. Go to back to bed," he insists, trumping my demand.

And, of course, I am obedient.

Chapter 8
The Aftermath

It's hard to be known as the family that lost its mother without eventually going in search of her.

"I've misplaced my mother," I chattered at night waiting for her to appear in my dream. "Like a sock, a mitten, or a key." I remember lying in bed, waiting for the familiar dream, feeling careless.

She stops at the corner of a busy street and glances at a very tall building. It seems to encroach onto the sidewalk. In fact, the street is like a narrow tunnel that tries to accommodate the hordes of people all walking with some urgency. I am behind her. I quickly follow the direction she is looking, but in that flash of a moment, she makes a quick turn. I've lost her. All I can see are the backs of bodies—heads of hair, one color. And then suddenly there is a bright spot of strawberry blonde. I try to hurry forward. My legs are incredibly heavy and I must grab each thigh to take a step. I am in slow motion. It is painful. I try to keep my eyes on her head, her brightly colored head. I try to yell to her. "Stop! Please! Over here!" But I make no sound. At the very moment I think I can't see her anymore, she turns around and looks at me full-faced. And even though I am almost a half-block away, I can see the color of her eyes. They are hazel, flecked with green or gray. Camouflage. And I know it's her.

When she disappears again I feel abandoned. I realize she knows who it is and leaves anyway. "How did you die?" I try to scream. "I'll let you go if you just tell me how you died."

Finally, the bottom-line. How did she die? The answer was the only way to leave the secret behind. To purge. The secret. (Could I then rehabilitate my memory?) Did my father kick her in the head and leave her for dead? Did he cause the rupture of that very fragile vein? Not intentionally. Of course not! How could a child think that? But in anger? He was angry that night. Humiliated in front of friends, one of whom was a business associate. I heard him say, "How could you embarrass me like that?" I heard that perfectly. But what had she done? Slurped her carbonara sauce? Had he dropped her too hard? Did her head hit the floor, or the side of the bed, or maybe the bureau? She was heavy. Understandable. An accident. But then she said, "Don't hurt me." Had he? Was he poised to do so? Was his fist raised? Or his foot. And his voice, was it hissing close to her ear when he discovered I was listening? Why did she say that, "Don't hurt me?" How compromised was she?

Why didn't I open the door?

Often I would look for evidence in that splotch on the carpet, the one she left behind, even after the soap, ammonia, and bleach spread it wider and deeper through the fibers of the wool, into the padding. I imagined even the floor was tinted a shade of red.

(Was it pimento? Persimmon? A berry medley or mousse? Curry, red cabbage, beets pickled in juice?)

Was it blood?

The stain created its own drop-off. My mind straddled its edges. I stalked it, knelt by its side, and smelled the fibers. I avoided stepping on it, like a freshly dug grave. Sometimes I became dizzy when I felt threatened by its pull and would lie on its edge, my lip tingling, until the darkness dissipated, waiting for a sign, from her, that there was nothing I could have done.

We had weathered four months of "firsts"—Mary's eighth birthday, my fourteenth, and Mom's thirty-eighth. My parents' sixteenth anniversary passed by on February fifteenth. Patty got her driver's license.

That spring, I entered Hawthorne Beauty Salon, swinging my ponytail one last time. It had taken a lifetime to grow, but the length held too much history. I couldn't look past my image without seeing my mother. There was no choice but to rid my forehead of the wave she crafted each morning in the exact width of her fingers; to eliminate the strong brush strokes that tamed my thick hair high on the back of my head; to dispose of the ribbons and elastics. I told John only to cut it short.

John thought I was effacing my mother's memory. How could I tell him that like the phantom kick of a stillborn, I felt her hand? And that I looked around for her then, waiting, always waiting, pretending she was alive. "Just cut it, John!" I think I screamed, at which point he grabbed some clumps, scissoring them off, leaving jagged ends.

The Queen of the May celebration came as usual that year. It was the Miss America contest for pubescent Catholic school girls. My class, the eighth graders at Saint Michael's, were responsible for electing a queen and her attendant (in the event she couldn't perform her duties). I was voted runner-up. The choice had little to do with religiosity. The event required that the two of us wear white dresses and gloves, hosiery, plus a tiara of flowers, to lead our classmates in a procession around Saint Michael's Church while praying the rosary. The culmination of the holy event was the solemn placement of a crown of flowers on the head of the BVM. With head bowed, clutching my rosary so that the crucifix dangled the divinely injured face forward, I followed the queen walking ten steps behind her as one of the nuns synchronized our movement with a soft handclap. Did I begin sobbing because my white shirtwaist was too small from all the double delight brownies the past four months? Or was it my ponytail, a missing appendage, which would have been braided with lilies of the valley? But it began when I placed my bouquet of spring flowers at the feet of the Blessed Virgin and looked up at her sweet smile. That was a first, too.

On Mother's Day, Mary gave me a card she had made in second grade. It said *With Love on Mother's Day.* In it she promised me the following spiritual bouquet: four Masses, four Holy Communions, eight visits to the Blessed Sacrament, three Rosaries, and fourteen Ejaculations. We went to dinner at The Heidelberg, a cozy family style restaurant where the specialty was wiener schnitzel and fried onion rings. It was the first time I heard my father mention my mother's death aloud when he chastised the waitress. Didn't she know that we were newly motherless and that he deserved better service from the bar? The waitress cried, and hurried for his Manhattan, Patty went to the ladies room returning with a scent of tobacco, and Mary knocked her silverware fitfully to the floor. I surreptitiously reached for her hand under the table. My father noticed.

"Don't ruin this dinner! I mean it. Wipe that look off your face."

I glanced at the tables around us, all that mother-breath inhaling the oxygen out of the room, and busied myself with distraction, distancing myself from the joylessness which would only anger my father further.

Summer came again. The warmth startled me after so many months of feeling chilled. Patty took Mom's place in the front seat as Memorial Day signaled our departure for the lake. There were no admonishments to use the bathroom that year as my father chugged his coffee and smoked while the car was being loaded. I sat behind him in the backseat and Mary behind Patty, balancing her sneakers on the picnic basket filled with peanut butter sandwiches, chips, and packaged cookies. Comics were no longer forthcoming from the front and none of us made our annual request to see the Tommy Bartlett Thrill Show at the Wisconsin Dells, the ice caves, or an Indian reservation. I felt unmoored by the establishment of new patterns. Patty chattered on. I glared at the back of her head for five hundred miles. My dad snarled about my sneer.

The El Rancho sign appeared in the distance. Its presence felt like an assault, as did the placard with the lake names. My father beeped the horn as we approached the cottages, the dust billowing behind us in a thick cloud, hordes of chipmunks diving into the ruts for cover. When our car turned up the slight slope before the cottage could be seen, I closed my eyes. I didn't want to see Mups standing there, her thin outline a little thinner, her apron tied with a precise knot, her pearl clip-ons and red lips. I didn't want to see her face when she bent down to peek in the front seat. I couldn't bear her look of sadness.

It was all as before—the cottage filled with mother. She was everywhere. The certain way the kitchen was arranged with cracked crockery perched on shelves, aprons hung on the back of a door, tablecloths stacked neatly in a hutch. I ran my hand over her old humpbacked chest where she stored our bedspreads and blankets in mothballs over the winter months. The top was stained from spilled nail polish remover the summer before. I looked on the back of her bedroom door and found her robe. A pair of tweezers and cherry red lipstick remained in the medicine cabinet. Her old sneakers were behind the cellar door.

Smells ran into one another—moth balls mingled with deep fat frying oil, perfume and mold, a general mustiness that was both acrid and lusty. Smells too alive. I opened every window and fled.

I walked the twenty-six steps down to the lake, slowly, deliberately, running my palm along the railing, ignoring the line of slivers marking my advancement. Dipping my feet into the water, I watched the ripples extend outward, circle after circle, until they diminished into the horizon. Only then did I notice the sweep of cool liquid pressing against my ankles. Lying on my stomach, I ran my fingers along the surface of the lake. I stared hard into its depths. I pretended she was there, hidden in the deep drop-offs with the lake gods. My lips brushed the water as I whispered my secret. I stared for a while into the clear water, and I waited. But only the blurred outline of my face stared back.

That summer, Patty and I started living a life without adult supervision, and except for the presence of Mups who treated us with benign tolerance, we had no boundaries. The two of us stayed in our cottage alone when our father went back to Chicago for weeks, while Mary spent most of her time with our grandparents next door. When Mups parked the Brown Bomber on the crest of our driveway, Patty and I would plan a nighttime exploit. (The Brown Bomber was one of the cars my grandfather purchased for summer driving after the men and their Chevrolets returned to the cities for work. It was a tank of a vehicle with rusted floorboards in the back which required complicated instructions from the adults on how to sit so as not to get sucked onto the road. Another was a yellow Nash Rambler, a pushbutton model in which the toggles for reverse and neutral had been popped into the dashboard, making for dizzying travel.)

Waiting until the lights went off next door (our exhaustion had our lights off much earlier!), we stared into the blackness for a while, and then bolted to the Bomber by way of the back door. As Patty released the brake, put the gear into neutral, jumped out, and helped me push it gently backwards, the car easily slipped onto the road. "Yikes," I muttered under my breath, watching Patty fly into the driver's seat as I climbed aboard. She was amazingly nimble from her years practicing to be a cheerleader.

That summer as we coasted down the road, this recklessness so-lidified our esprit de corps. We were giddy with grief and uncon-cerned about consequences. Silence sat between us. I don't know why I didn't trust Patty with what I knew—didn't share the burden, bonding both of us by the treacherous truth instead of by silence. I really didn't know how to begin. "Uh, Patty," I practiced. "Ummm, I think Dad…" But I couldn't get past the *Ummm*, capturing the urge in a never-ending holding pattern, inevitably sparing her the details.

We flew around the countryside in that car, sometimes running off the road into cornfields, having to explain to Mups the next day why there were shucks in the backseat. We stopped in pool halls on different lakes where we hung out like escapees. We drank and smoked and cursed. We kissed the boys and hoped to god we didn't run into any one of them in Cold Spring where we shopped at Pe-ter's Grocery each week. We fabricated stories about ourselves, more palatable than reality. Early in the morning, we returned to the lake by the light of the moon, stealthily parking the Brown Bomber in its usual place, and slept all morning until Mups insisted we come over for breakfast.

"What's wrong with you girls?" she'd laugh. "You'd think you were out carousing all night!"

And because Mups had us convinced she was a psychic, we were a little worried she might read our faces for signs of our illicit behavior. I remember her studying tea leaves splayed on the side of her Havilland china (simple cream-colored cups with light roses and green thorny stems) during our prior vacations. She and my mother would sit side by side dropping a teaspoonful of loose tea into the cup followed by hot water in anticipation of good news.

Mups told me once that she saw strange lights—auras, she called them. She saw one surrounding my mother's crib one morning. I asked her if it was like a halo surrounding a saint's head, a nimbus cloud of golden rays. (I so wanted her to say "yes!")

It was duller than that, Mups said, with an odor of roses. In fact, it was the smell that attracted her to the room so early in the morning.

"You know how smell evokes memories," Mups said. "There was something in that rose smell that stirred my emotions, but there were no memories involved. It rooted me to the spot in the doorway. I couldn't move or speak. I was barely breathing, and I stayed that way until it vanished."

"And then what?" I whispered. "What did you do then?"

But her memory was clogged. Like mine. Maybe it was genetic.

(I found a bottle of Chanel Number 5 among my mother's cosmetics, a half-filled bottle which I held to my nose after Mups told me this story. I waited for a bit of clarity, just enough for me to seize a glimmer of her. Unfortunately, like Mups, nothing was forthcoming, except a hint of a headache.)

But Mups didn't need to read tea leaves that summer to ferret out the underbelly of our feelings. We were all broken, the four of us. Mups became more drawn as the summer wore on, and I couldn't help thinking that we must have reminded her daily of the loss she incurred, as did Mups to me. As much as I wanted her to be a surrogate mother, she couldn't offer me the security I needed to share my story, my secret life. She drew a boundary with humor and flippancy, avoiding circumspection. So, again, my mother's death was not mentioned. It was almost as if Mups believed she had succeeded in distracting us from our loss.

"If we don't talk about it, then it isn't there."

I admit, I felt cheated by her fragility and her fear, if that is what caused her restraint. I craved an adult.

When my father returned to the lake, Grandma vanished to her sister Olivia's house.

"I'm unable to take full breaths," she sighed. "Maybe it's just the dog days of summer. The air is so still. I feel like I'm suffocating. Let's go to town and pick some Glads."

And off we went in the Brown Bomber to Olivia's home, through fields of corn so high that only the top of the old car could be seen.

"We look like an enormous beetle," Grandma tittered. "I'll bet the farmers are terrified."

A visit to Aunt Olivia's garden was the perfect antidote to my father's visits which left us all anxious and wary. It was a mosaic of colors and a maze of paths through asters, delphiniums, anemones, and black-eyed Susan. But she was famous for her Glads. Olivia carried her "sharp snips" as she called them, in her apron, along with a mixture of eggshells and coffee grounds for fertilizing. During our trip back to the lake, Grandma told me how much she admired the sturdy Gladioli.

"Glads are the brightest of funeral flowers," she said, her face brightening a bit. "They live a long time during the dreadful ordeal and look cheerful on the casket and afterwards in the cemetery. Did you know they mean remembrance?"

Then she and I unloaded bushels full of the flowers, and arranged them in buckets lining one path, main cottage to the altar of BVM, a funeral path it seemed to me, a path of swords. She wouldn't remove them until my father headed back to Chicago, even if the flowers were dead by that time.

That first summer, my grandfather bought every Mass offering that was available at the farm church in Jacob's Prairie where we went to services each Sunday. He also donated large sums of money to their annual Harvest Festival, the "Pork Chop and Corn on the Cob Feed" that the parish hosted every August. Saint James Church printed my mother's name in their bulletin under the column "In Memory" from Memorial Day to Labor Day, reminding us of our motherless status, lest we forget. Grandpa had a reason for his generosity: he was purchasing indulgences from each parishioner for her release from purgatory, if that was where she was. Indulgenced prayers were sentence fragments, really, where you invoked the names of the many saints who might intervene on behalf of the dead person for a swift release from purgatory. The totality of the prayer was simply, "Saint Agatha save the soul of *insert name*. Saint Theresa save the soul of *insert name*." The number of Saints you invoked was directly related to the number of days removed from the totality of suffering in purgatory. In actual numbers then, if the punishment was five hundred years, a couple hundred days could be knocked off in a matter of minutes. If the prayers were recited privately, an indulgence of three years was granted, but if spoken publicly, five years. And who said God wasn't merciful? Hell, however, was a different animal altogether. There was no way out of Hell.

There were no shortcuts in the ritual. After each saint's name, you had to add "save our soul," or "their souls," or "pray for us," or "them," or "have peace on her, him, them, us," or other equally relevant requests. In other words, running through a list of saints and adding an "SOS" on the end didn't count. Sometimes during weekly school Mass, one of the priests would read a list of names deemed good for an indulgence, and we would try to keep up with the refrain. The nuns would manage the synchronization of our voices by clicking their pocket clickers, small pieces of metal which made a cricket type sound.

"Saint Ignatius," click-ick "pray for us."

"Saint Patrick," click-ick "pray for us."

"Saint Peter," click-ick "pray for us."

Only their clicking was pretissimo. "SainIgnaclickickprayforusSssPatclickickPrayforusSPeclickickPrayforus," our voices eventually overrun by the cacophony of cricket sounds. We learned back in our classrooms that our demeanor essentially erased any time off for the poor souls in purgatory.

I dreamt noisily that first summer, with Patty on one side and the demonic electrical box on the other. My unconscious kept playing a discordant symphony, something from Stravinsky, I think, maybe *The Rite of Spring*. One night, in the middle of the second movement, just when the percussionists become infatuated with their importance—I heard the gentlest tinkle, from a triangle maybe, or the beginning of a rain, a few drops and then a quick shower, ceasing as suddenly as it had begun, leaving only the squeaking of worn bedsprings behind. It wasn't Stravinsky at all but the flow and ebb of my father so inebriated that he warped the boards in the corner of his bedroom with the diluted splash of his Perfect Manhattan, over the Sacre du Printemps of a late summer's night dream.

"This is what I missed," he said as they spooned in the summer breeze.

It was a first summer for him as well.

Even after he chased Patty through the gully, down one side and up the other screaming "Slut!" I was embarrassed rather than hateful, especially after he slipped and rolled down the slippery slope of moist soil towards the center where the terrain segued into a natural fire pit. Besides, my father behaved towards us as if we were out to deceive him, to do irrevocable damage to his good name. I'm afraid he believed in the whore-mother—where women were the seductresses (and men were studs!). In his eyes, there were good girls or bad girls, the former being passive and pure, a Mary Ann not a Ginger, a BVM, rather than a Magdalen. Catholicism absolved bad boy behavior. It was up to us, the temptresses, to protect the opposite sex from sin. After all, we were the ones with the clothing, speech, make-up, smiles, winks, wiggles, giggles, touch, breath, perfume, and god forbid, kisses, that led to hell.

"It is up to you to stop the boys!" the nuns would lecture us in religion classes. "You have more strength. More self-control. More responsibility."

They never added that we had a womb that could swell like a balloon. But my father was keenly aware of the side effect of momentary bliss.

"Don't get pregnant!" he'd say aloud when we left for dates, when we hiked to the park, rode our bicycles to school, roller-skated, ice-skated, talked on the phone, visited girlfriends. Did he despise that part of us; the part that got him married? And what *about* that? The married part. Did he feel trapped, especially after he became saddled with three girls? Did he look at our maturing physical selves and feel powerless?

My father didn't hurt himself when he slipped down the hill, although it must have been astonishing to the relatives that were assembled around a small campfire that night. If my father had rolled a few years before, he not only would have suffered from poison ivy, but also would likely have been cut on the glass and metal that had been discarded in the gully for decades. Patty and I knew—we had raked it for two years, making it look like the backdrop for a Norman Rockwell painting of which my father was fond. This particular evening could have been captured on canvas as *Besotted by Moonlight,* and except for the father tumbling towards a fire, passed for a scene of Americana. My grandfather was watching from his cottage next door, perhaps planning his own oil painting minus the fire and the people. Most likely Gramps would have been smiling at this debacle, his expectations having been met by my father for familial failure, of which my sisters and I were becoming the victims. Wasn't he alarmed by all this chaos? Did he and Mups ever discuss an intervention? Were they ever inspired to do something more than just witness how adept we were becoming at surviving? Why *were* we left to our own devices?

My father landed within inches of the fire to the sound of a collective "Sheesh" from the assembled relatives. "Wha'll staring at?" he condensed, brushing the gray ash from his hairy arms. He managed this with some panache, too, making sure that his posture was erect while taking measured steps to the path that would take him from our house to the altar of the BVM where he was sure Patty was hiding by now.

His two sisters who were visiting for the first, and last time, managed to start a rather wobbly third verse of "On Top of Old Smoky" after it was certain my father had cleared the area. It didn't surprise me that there were no questions, no comments. There never were. Who wanted to open Pandora's Box? (Although I always hoped I could be coaxed.) And anyway, I knew what was under his ashy skin that night because I smelled it too when Patty ran by. It was her fragrance, my mother's, and I was sure that if I turned slowly enough, I would catch her broad toothy smile surrounded by Honest to God red lipstick—a figure standing there in pedal pushers and a crisp white blouse, smoking a cigarette, her arm linked with Grandma's. Maybe she'd just had her palm read, and her lifeline was longer than ever, a line that traveled down her palm and connected all of us to her. A mother-line of steel. But of course, it wasn't her at all, but her favorite fragrance, Prince Matchabelli, embedded in her sweater, the faded blue cashmere that Patty had grabbed from a hook by the back door.

This was his inebriated self, his impatient self, his I don't want to be a father and be responsible for your behavior self. This was the "I don't believe a word you are saying" self, the "I know what girls do" self, the "No way will you embarrass me" self. Because his own marriage with my mother was hastily arranged after she found herself pregnant with Patty, his reaction may have been directed more towards my mother. (A smoldering rant did seem to persist right under the radar with us, my sisters and me. Why would my mother have been treated differently?) If the lingering odor of her perfume hadn't been so pervasive, he might not have become so disoriented by his fury.

As I watched the performance, I couldn't help but think he suffered from the "I hate myself" self.

Patty didn't stick around to see if the hate he might have had for himself would continue to spill over onto her. She decided to move out after that incident even though my father couldn't articulate what it was that he was chasing that night. She made her arrangements when we returned to Chicago, that first week in September, before her seventeenth birthday.

"It's final," she announced. "I'm going to a friend's house. It's all arranged. My mind cannot be changed. I can't live here anymore."

That was when my father pulled out the *AA* pamphlets, addressing our hope and prayers—one with the philosophy and the other with testimonials. I'm fairly certain he never attended any meetings. At least he didn't in the evening. He was home, loaded every night. And as long as I had ever known him, he had only alluded to a higher power once, on the day of my mother's death, and maybe again when our pastor, Father Kirk, perished in a rectory fire.

Maybe somebody would have taken a closer look at the family if Patty had fled. Girls didn't leave their families then, at least girls didn't leave if unmarried, and barely seventeen. Would this person (this savior!) have wormed their way through this breach in the family facade? Would we have been rescued? And my father. What would have transpired for him? If forced by our departure, would he have been able to assess his life and ours, the three girls, absent the scrim of alcohol?

It wasn't like me to be optimistic, yet I encouraged Patty to remain to see if our father could live up to his promises. Just for a while, *please,* although as frightened as I was to be left with him, alone, I was ambivalent. I knew she was advocating for herself, that she would have been better off. Her attempt to leave was incredibly brave, and one that he, dear old dad, put in his quiver to shoot her with as necessary.

By the fall of that year, the illusion of *AA* and sobriety gave way to our garage wall through which my father plowed his car straight into the family room. He had abandoned our Chevy sometime in the spring of 1963 and purchased a Pontiac Grand Prix. I had to admit it was pretty cool with bucket seats, padded dash, and four on the floor, yet I couldn't help feeling unfaithful, especially when Gramps saw it that summer.

My grandfather ran across the gully as soon as he noticed the interloper, calling it a "son of a bitchin car" (not a compliment) causing a fine spray of spittle to settle conspicuously across the new finish. To my father's credit, he responded without a word, swiped at the hood with his folded hankie, and grabbed a beer from a cooler in the backseat. Gramps' scarlet scalp radiated danger through his white crown of hair as he held one hand under each armpit. Patty and I scattered.

I assumed there was an attempt made at some point to brake the vehicle before contact with the concrete wall, although everything was accelerating by then, his drinking, his driving, his sudden fits of anger. He had hung six tennis balls from the ceiling for just such a braking eventuality, in case he forgot, which he had in the past, judging from the moderate dents which peppered the garage. They were strategically placed, nanoseconds between, hitting the driver's side window first, and then the roof— *plunkplunkplunkplunkplunk-plunk*. When that didn't fully suffice as a warning, he nailed railroad ties to the concrete floor spanning the entire width of the garage. Apparently in the wee hours of this Saturday morning, the last *plunk* of a tennis ball or railroad tie could not prevail.

The scraped and dented Pontiac left a perfect cutout in the paneling. One light was shattered, the grill was dented, and the hood ornament, a shiny black *GP*, lay on the brown flecked linoleum of the family room. Oil slowly dripped and formed a rivulet that my sisters and I followed that morning towards the kitchen. We ate our breakfast on its hood, and because the top was down, watched Saturday morning cartoons from the front seat. (Didn't everyone live this way?) The burgundy Pontiac Grand Prix was the elephant bleeding in the family room, and true to the metaphoric image, never discussed, not even when backing it through the hole in the family room wall required arm motions from the three of us stationed on either side of the car.

After that, I began to worry more than usual about the people, *entire families,* my father might encounter while driving drunk. The potential of him maiming, paralyzing, actually killing with his vehicle made me feel partially responsible, because I knew what he was capable of under the influence.

Each morning before school, I combed the local newspaper to see if there were any hit-and-run accidents in the western suburbs of Chicago. I plucked the day-old *Chicago Sun Times* from the garbage and looked for dead people other than those found emanating foul odors from abandoned cars which dotted the Chicago landscape. (Sometimes I got distracted. There were quite a few murders during my years of research, especially amid the summer months. The Mafia boss, Sam Giancana, "Momo" he was called, plus Sam Battaglia were industrious during heat waves and their brutalities were detailed news. And then there was Richard Speck who murdered eight student nurses in Chicago.) I ran my hand over the flanks of his Pontiac checking for dents. When he went to the Gables Bar on the edge of town, I waited for the phone to ring with the bad news. If he stopped on Friday nights at Andy's Family Steakhouse for a cocktail, I hoped none of my friends were there enjoying a T-bone with their families. I preferred for him to drink at home, with his car keys safely in the pewter dish which was inscribed with a toast, "Health, Wealth, Happiness, and the Time to Enjoy Them," sitting by the front door.

As I worried, unwelcome thoughts were accompanied by inane activity. It became a slippery slope. Are the doors locked, is the stove off, light switches completely down, or up? (A middle stage might cause a short.) What about the coffee pot, the stereo, the iron? If I didn't remove the iron and feel the end of the plug, I wasn't sure. I imagined objects flushed and beaming, waiting to replug themselves. Uncertainty reigned about doors being locked, keys being lost, dryers starting fires, washers flooding. After I began driving, a bump in the road became a body. I would return to the scene of the figmental crime and look for the injured, the maimed, the dead. I associated myself so deeply with my father's recklessness, potential outcomes became my reality. I now realize that I was trying to diminish the anxiety created by my father's unpredictability, but at that time, my brain was on overload from this compulsive activity competing with the secret.

The truth was my father knew he was a drunk driver. His method of driving defensively was complete inebriation. "No, I don't worry about drunk drivers," he laughed, setting my teeth on edge. "I'm always the drunkest!"

(Could it get any worse?)

It was as if he were vindictive toward a world that had treated him wrongly from the very first, a world that wasn't nearly as bright, as capable, and as talented as he saw himself. And the worst part of all, he didn't care, not in the least. He was entitled. And aggrieved.

I searched for a patron saint for my father; a patron for drinking, or drinking too much, even drinking while driving. After all, there were patron saints for mad dogs, and fear of mice, taxi drivers, dysentery, and whales, surely there was one for alcohol. A trilogy of prayer was required—for the cocktail hour, to guide him through the course of his hangover, and for safety while he drank his "roadies." Matt Talbott was the only name I could come up with, an Irishman who began drinking at the age of twelve. Unfortunately, Matt could not complete the assignments needed for canonization. "He needs a few more miracles," Father Lynch told me after I inquired during catechism. ("My friend has an uncle, Father. Or maybe it's her cousin.")

"Why don't you tell her to pray to Saint Theresa, the Little Flower instead?"

I decided to try my mother's approach even though it hadn't turned out all that well for her. I settled on a novena. I finally succumbed to Saint Jude, the Saint of Hopeless cases.

"Dear Saint Jude," I said. "I apologize for having offended thee in any way. Please take the keys away from my father when he leaves the Gables Bar, Andy's Steakhouse, Rush Street in Chicago, the Palmer House, the White Hall Club, Old Town, The Drake's Cape Cod Room, and Green Door Tavern. Please give him the strength to resist the canted martini glasses in the window at Club Lucky. And if he has to drink, make it a Schlitz and make it only one. Amen." (Times nine.)

I tried to be all-inclusive and then worried about my culpability in the event I left out one of his drinking establishments. I added an addendum requiring Saint Jude to use his own judgment and thanked him in advance. My prayers were answered. As far as I knew, my father never killed anyone. At least not on the road.

That fall I assuaged my guilt and grief at the local VFW. Friday night fish fries with French fries and fried onion rings and fried chicken (if you weren't Catholic) topped off with a double delight brownie. Invited out of sincerity and concern, I joined a vet family each Friday, my double-delight family, a family that couldn't imagine "blanch," "scald," or "poached," attributed to any food. Eventually I didn't bother to change my school uniform, my tidy skirt with sewn down pleats. I just ate and ate and ate until my skirt popped its stitching, became a dirndl, and my mouth had a suspicious brown rim.

I spent the rest of that winter and early spring the following year burrowing from the world into my own layers of fat. (A secret here, a secret there, by god I grew out of my underwear.)

Then Mups arrived in her high heels, seamed silk hosiery, fox stole, straight skirt, and veiled hat. By the time she left, I had a Chubbette dress and an eating disorder. The catalyst for my dip into anorexia was nothing more than a second hard roll covered in sesame seeds with a single pat of butter squeezed in the middle. We were at Bonwit Teller, at a lingerie fashion show, Mups and I, "to catch up," she said, "to see how you are doing." It probably was indelicate to mention the VFW fish fry while surrounded by lithesome nymphs in clouds of gauzy fabric. Or to go on about the double delights.

Mups spent an inordinate amount of time poking and prodding my shirt into the waistband of my skirt, straightening my collar, brushing something imaginary from my shoulder, over and over, before we were even seated at our table. I wondered if she had developed some sort of tic since I saw her last. The drumming of her fingers on the white linen began with my first hard roll and came to a halt as I reached for one more starchy lump.

"Another one?" she asks archly.

"I guess not," I gulp, my face beet red, a perfect match with her suspended nails.

"Try your salad," Mups chirps, more like her sweet self. "It will fill you up nicely. You'll see. And some berries for dessert. They will be wonderful."

Records hung on the same hanger with each Chubbette dress, skirt, capri pant, and blouse in the preteen department. ("Your chubby lass can be belle of her class!") They were the lure to Slim Girl Fashions designed by Jackie Mayer, Miss America 1963. The label on the record said, "Slim Along with Jackie Mayer," and without ever putting needle to groove, I hung my red plaid Chubbette dress in my closet and peeked at it only when I was in danger of falling off the wagon. *I'll show you, Mups*, I thought. "I can lose my undies too. I will fit in the shadow of Uncle Louie's derriere before I'm done." I learned to eat fewer than five hundred calories per day, substituting all meals for one sweet roll shaped in a perfect figure eight with a dollop of cream cheese in each oval and a bit of lemon zest. A single roll would sit in the cupboard on one of my mother's blue "Poppycock" plates, sliced methodically into tiny pieces, the cream cheese eventually scraped away because of its dense caloric content. The more weight I lost, the more powerful I felt. For once I was in control of something. And strangely, I felt full.

At dinner my food landed in paper napkins after a good bit of chewing. My father wasn't lucid enough after his third pitcher of Perfect Manhattans to notice the sequence of chew and swipe. But even so, my sisters and I were professionals having removed years of troublesome meals with a delicacy of manners. (We were not allowed to leave the table without eating everything on our plates due to the starving children in China. It was the Catholic way, and no amount of gagging could change this precept.) Beets, Aunt Ella's goulash, stuffed green peppers, creamed peas, and oyster stew, all masticated to an indecipherable lump. It was an almost perfect system unless the rare occasion called for linen.

There were no temptations, even from our kitchen pantry, as it was slowly divested of food I enjoyed. After a while, all that I noticed were jars of olives—interesting olives—Nicoise style, sun-dried olives, some, called fiery hot devils, stuffed with a chili pepper. There were Greek olives, Italian olives, some cracked, others a dull green, smoked, or bobbing in white wine. They were stuffed with almonds, anchovies, mushrooms, and onions, floating in brine and garlic. I alphabetized them once, as my mother did her spices, and then gave them to our Catholic church one winter for a holiday food drive—except for the Red Hot Mama's which I fully intended to taste when I reached eighty-nine pounds. My palate stung for days.

My two sisters eventually became anorectics as well, counting, measuring, denying, controlling, obsessing, being perfect. We competed. Goaded each other. We still do.

"Here, Patty, your favorite. Some chips and dip."

"Mary! Frosted brownies!"

"Mickey, another doughnut? They're small. One hundred calories tops!"

We could have created a sibling or two from our cast-off poundage. And then we noticed a few of our cousins were thinning out as well. Had Mups created this legacy of starving females? Were we trying to disappear? Or immolate the demons that inhabited our interior lives? (Didn't everyone have a personal monster?) Or were we simply trying to fit the image of flawlessness as prescribed by our environment?

In the end, this fulfillment of deprivation carved a void so profound that I found the abyss almost impossible to ascend from. But for a while at least, the stars which appeared in front of my eyes clouded my reality, providing some momentary relief.

Before the year was out my father had joined The Men's Club at Saint Mark's Parish, a collection of disbelievers who were coddled and cared for as those with special spiritual needs until such time they could be mainstreamed into the general fold. They drank, smoked, and played cards in the name of Our Lord, on the first Saturday night of each month. When it came to his own salvation, my father hoped that God had a sense of humor, and otherwise relied on Father Kirk, for entertainment. I was heartened until Father Kirk died following one of those first Saturdays, further refuting the possibility that God possessed a funny bone. The next Saturday, my father went to confession, only the second time I ever remember him partaking of absolution. I became troubled over the possibility of a budding modus operandi.

The rectory was a few blocks from our home. It was an old stone building and unfortunately its interior was highly volatile, having had years of varnish coated on every window ledge, doorframe, and cabinet. Plus there were old church bulletins stashed everywhere. Sirens roared through the sleeping neighborhood early in the morning around three or four a.m., startling me from a dream about my mother being delivered back to her bedroom floor. My best friend Linda called me at dawn to report school had been cancelled because the rectory had burned down from a smoldering cigarette. Her youngest brother's namesake, the pastor, had been killed. I thought of my father who had been playing cards over there the night before. I wanted to ask if the cigarette had been found. Was it a Kent or a Camel? Menthol or Regular? Filtered or Unfiltered? I didn't want the notoriety of fraternizing with the priest killer.

Someone reported later that by the time the rectory exploded, toxic fumes had already killed Father Kirk. Rumor had it that he must have dreamt he was in church smelling acrid incense and never awakened. I guessed that was supposed to provide us some consolation, the notion that he died without regaining his wits. No one mentioned it was the morning after the first Saturday of the Men's Club. My father never said a thing and avoided joining another organization.

Patty and I had to find another priest for our weekly confession after that nasty fire chewed through everything edible in the rectory. We had taken to shoplifting by then. Lord and Taylor was our favorite target. Stacks of cashmere sweaters in fuchsia, yellow, and bright blue beckoned us. We gathered them in hefty piles, too numerous to count, and emerged from the dressing room with our skinny little bodies plumper, and certainly healthier looking.

"No thank you," we would smile at the clerk handing her our rejects. "This one just isn't the right color. This one, too large. I already have this color at home." And off we would toddle, fingering everything in sight until we reached the door.

I worried about this breach of morality in the dead of night. If I died, I would go to Hell, no questions asked, my last breath riding the swoosh of my soul plummeting to the netherworld—the big gooey mortal sin as its anchor. I was clearly a novice. Before this, I had only shoplifted a ten-pack of Bazooka from the Pik 'n Sav, and only once. I was sorry, too! Heartily. And made a beeline to confession, choosing the visiting priest who wouldn't recognize my voice.

The visiting priest always had the longest line; it snaked around the altar and aisle and was comprised of people who preferred someone other than their parish priest. The queue formed close enough to the confessional door so that a murmur could be heard, as well as the sound of the sliding screen as the priest pivoted from side to side in his little closet, sinner to sinner, back and forth, giving blessings and doling out penance. When it was my turn to enter the confessional, it took a moment to adapt to the complete darkness and the slight depression in the kneeler as I slipped onto my knees. I could picture the light blinking on and off outside the door as I adjusted myself. It probably looked like a distress signal. "Bazooka!" I imagined spelling in Morse Code to the waiting line. "Bazooka! Bazooka! Bazooka!" My hands automatically covered my nose as I smelled the sweat, gas, and peppermint gum left by the last poor soul—then I added another sin to my list for impure thoughts. When the screen slid back to reveal the profile of the priest, I began, (as quietly as possible) naming my sins and enumerating their frequency since my last confession. I spoke fast and intermittently cleared my throat, managing to slip the Bazooka Gum between being mean to my sisters and disobeying my parents. I received penance, absolution, a blessing, and the Bazooka caper became part of my death video. I exited lighter, freer, worthy of Heaven, or at the minimum, a brief stint in Purgatory, the holding pen for a bit more suffering. That was the beauty of confession. It was the antidote to being seven or eight or nine years old. Normal developmental milestones became sins. The sins were confessed. I was saved from Hell for another week.

Father Kirk always blessed us too, with an admonishment to return the sweaters, or dresses, or blouses, "at once!" or to reimburse the store for the correct amount. He always added an addendum to our penance in order for us to illustrate our sincerity, frequently amounting to a donation to the church. Wracked with guilt and anxiety, I usually ended up doing all three, but only after wearing my new wardrobe a few times.

I think Father Kirk knew who we were. I don't think priests were above sneaking a peak at the sinner through the filmy grill, but even if he didn't look, Patty and I were frequent visitors pleading for mercy and kindness and understanding. He couldn't miss the pattern in our recitation, *"one red sweater and a white blouse to wear underneath"* or our strong and sincere self-flagellation. But I guess the priestly privilege prevented him from delving into our depravity just a little, to try and figure out what we were trying to assuage besides the chill in the air.

In the fall of 1965, I decided I had to remove myself from my father's scorn. I was sixteen. My mother had been dead for less than three years. Patty was attending the College of Saint Mary's at Notre Dame where my father was visiting for a football weekend. Mary was with an aunt. And me? I was dropping out of school.

He leans on the horn announcing his arrival. I look out the window from my parents' room. It is Ray. We have been dating for a year. He is eighteen, a senior at Saint Francis High School for the second time. A scholar he isn't. He throws his talent into football. They will miss him on the field next weekend, I think.

I am running away. A southern state. Few questions. We talked about getting married. Ray has a car, an old Checker Cab. The dome light is turned on.

My red vinyl suitcase sits by the front door. Among a few sweaters, I have packed my glow-in-the-dark rosary, some books, photos of my sisters, and of course, the secret.

After months of planning I am suddenly paralyzed. I look over at the red stain, barely decipherable. Its edges waver. The horn starts bleating again and then sharp rapping at the front door. There is something in his insistence that is irritating.

I walk into the interior of the house. Sliding down the wall, I hug myself until my muscles ache. A neighbor has approached my boyfriend, my betrothed! All is quiet.

My consciousness stopped revolving if only for a moment and thankfully birthed one concisely drawn thought. The unknown may not be better. The need to escape morphed from father to Ray.

You don't need to leave right now. Don't do it.

I called Uncle Bob, the car dealer. He had developed a personal dislike for my father ever since his defection from Chevy to Pontiac and seemed the perfect choice for a rescue.

Bob was a gentleman, he was inarticulate, and he was perceptive. There weren't any questions about the heaviness of my suitcase, the multiple maps mostly of Southern states that I carried to the trash, about the phone ringing continuously. It was enough that I had requested a break, a respite so to speak, from having to make Manhattans.

My uncle spoke to my father. He and Aunt Shirley were willing to have me live with them. I remember being relieved. And tired.

My collection of Edgar Allen Poe stories and small cloth-bound works of Shakespeare were unpacked and back on my shelf within thirty-six hours after an effective bribe by my father of weekly *AA* meetings, two tickets to the Ice Capades, plus a fifty-dollar bill. He wasn't above a little padding. Besides there was Mary. Feeling like a traitor and keeping secrets at Uncle Bob's was more tiring than stirring cocktails and surviving a skirmish each night. My father's quiver grew heavier.

How could I remain in this domicile with this man, my father, whose personality changed between pitchers? Who frightened me with his temper? Who twisted my words in the best of times, into a form I didn't recognize in the worst? I was dependent on someone I was beginning to loathe. Patty reluctantly helped me look for an apartment when she returned from college. I scoured local newspapers for employment near my high school, to build a nest egg. I was determined that I wouldn't live my life as a hostage because I didn't have my own checkbook. I became employed selling Jean Paree wigs and wiglets at Bonwit Teller. I soon discovered that peddling the lifelike heads sitting on padded limbs with pageboys, bubbles, pixies, and extensions was distressing. A few of the severed heads looked like Jackie-O, with the pillbox hat, strand of pearls, classic bangs, dark ringed eyes. I could almost hear her wispy voice, "And this is where I redecorated with a Prussian Blue." The heads began to take on personalities, which I tried to accommodate with the correct hairstyle. A bob for the flighty; the pixie for the childish; pageboys were the bluebloods; and the French twist—my mother. Besides, Patty told me I was being short-sighted. "Two more years, you dunce! Two more and you get out of the house for college! It's worth it."

Patty did seem to be thriving. Would I survive two more years? Weight was slipping off my frame so fast, maybe I would just vanish. Poof! Would my father even notice? And my grades. They were pitiful. I was unsure I could even get admitted to college. Certainly not Saint Mary's where Patty attended, and later Mary. That door was closed. I already knew that. I listened to Patty and abandoned my plan, leaving the mannequins *tsssking* behind my abrupt departure.

Romantic firsts came and went for my father as well, beginning with one brief fling with a woman named Isabelle. She was short, had large breasts, green eyes, and wore her hair in a French twist. She loved music boxes and gave me one that played the theme from *Dr. Zhivago*. It had a Russian girl decoupaged on the lid. Isabelle had a daughter younger than my sisters and me. My father said there was no way he was going to do that one more time—raise another girl.

"Besides, I can drink when I want," he said. "Why would I get married again? Give up my freedom? Have someone telling me what I cannot do?"

He probably told Isabelle that the memory of his departed wife prevented further conjugal relationships. Isabelle should have been thankful. She was able to avoid the pall of the errant cerebrum.

Then came the men, but only after he had abandoned the family home and all its memories on Hawthorne Boulevard.

They arrived at the Astor House, my father's fancy apartment on the Gold Coast, with covered parking and balconies (no door man though). They came with their firm gazes and solid bodies in shades of off-white.

Was my father expanding his repertoire of friends to include those that he had heretofore considered beneath him? Didn't he notice there was a Spaniard, a Cuban, and a Korean accessing his apartment? They were never passed off as long-lost uncles either, or colleagues from exotic regions of the fabric industry, classmates, childhood friends, or foreign diplomats. They were just, well, there, at separate times, one supplanting the next.

One of them made pillows for my father's summer home in Minnesota. They were gold and black with a subdued toucan on the front of each. When they were lined up along the perimeter of my father's conversation pit—a narrow, long bench flanking a fireplace—the birds appeared to be kissing each other. There had to be forty of them, placed in this vertiginous pattern. Jacinto sewed each one with a few bolts of material from Sears and my mother's sewing machine after he arrived from Valencia. He tried to make an English garden in the Big Fish Lake landscape with walkways through indigenous plants fertilized with fish carcasses and scales. He cooked and cleaned and helped with the housework. Jacinto was part of the British consulate in Chicago. We thought he might be royalty. My sisters and I actually liked him. He talked about his mother. We imagined his friendship with my father being tied somehow to foreign travel. My father was civilized around him.

Ky Juoung worked at the Ambassador East in Chicago as a chef. I am certain he wasn't famous for his culinary prowess. He had a family and a couple of kids. My father invited him to Patty's home a few times after she had married and he spent the majority of his time perseverating over the pattern in her stoneware dishes. He thought they were embedded with dirt. She usually prepared Chung King Chow Mein or Chung King Chop Suey served over Uncle Ben's Rice. My father began shouting, "Stop it!" halfway through the meal whenever Ky Juoung rubbed his thumbnail across a dish

"The spots won't come off on your chop suey. Damn it! Don't worry."

But, Jacinto and Ky Juoung were benign compared to Raymundo. Raymundo was from Cuba. He spent his time either in my father's bedroom or fixed in the open doorway, his hands and feet in respective corners cast like an X. He had a proprietary air about him, never spoke to any of us, and treated my sisters and me as if we had stumbled into the wrong apartment. We were sure he was after family assets, what else could it be? It was impossible for us to think it was love. Was it? Between these men? How could they get past their foreboding temperaments to experience anything but hostility? Sometimes Raymundo would bolt from the bedroom without looking sideways, out the door into the hallway where he punched the elevator call button with his index finger until it opened to the astonished, mostly Jewish residents of Astor House. And then he would place his body in the same X-shape he employed in our apartment, just for a moment, defying anyone to demand he let the elevator resume.

My father's reputation took a definite slide in the Astor House when Raymundo was around, so much so that our collective perkiness couldn't dispel the gloom of the residents.

Was this where his anger germinated? The man stuck in the middle of desire and denial? A product of the 1950s which declared homosexuality an illness, but one that could be cured? By marriage? And three girls? A dead wife? And Perfect Manhattans? But what do I know for sure about this. Except the stink of his anger.

Creighton University in Omaha admitted me on a probationary status. Their enrollment must have needed some bolstering. Mups lived in Omaha then, and even though she would be felled by the light fixture by the end of my sophomore year, we saw each other occasionally, and talked more than that, nothing too deep. After all, I was thin, which in her book exemplified health.

My father called the dorm every Sunday after Mary had stirred his first pitcher. By the time the conversation ended, he was well into his cups. If I sounded too happy, he thought I wasn't working hard enough. If my mood was serious, I was ungrateful by being unhappy. It was my Sunday dinner of crazy salad, no calories, just heartburn. Often he told me he would pull the plug on my tuition, especially after I declared my intention to become a social worker. (He was always worried about my desire to become a pediatrician. In his mind, no good could ever came of a young girl being so infatuated with babies. But a social worker was pretty close to communism.)

"I'm not paying for graduate school! You'll need a job at the end of four years. Who do you think you are? And what do you think I am?! A money tree? Anyway, you're just going to get married."

Which is exactly what I did after two and a half years of sitting in a phone booth paying my dues, right after Patty, who married the same year.

Chapter 9
Facing the Demons

As the secret and I matured, we found ourselves observing my father, wondering how he would cope if he *were* responsible. We tried to detect self-hatred, perturbed sleep, weight loss, isolation. We tried to sense penance; nervousness. I sniffed the air for fear when we were together. I justified his anger with me as a fear of loss of control. Over me. I wondered if he imagined me as a threat, or if he, too, regretted that I didn't enter their bedroom that night.

(You know that I know. I could turn you in. I have power. Your reputation is in my hands.)

Maybe all I wanted was for him to simply apologize for his disinterest in how *that night* became the prelude to so many days stacked like pancakes, without dimension.

This occasional headiness, however, was rooted in wistfulness rather than reality. His behavior simply didn't change towards me over the course of our relationship: father-daughter, predator-witness, defense-prosecution. Understandably, I coveted the fathers of my friends, siphoning the characteristics I craved, fashioning a loving male mentor, a confidante, a role model—my illusive progenitor.

I did feel sympathy for him, maybe even pity, as I grew into adulthood. I understood that the loss of a spouse under any circumstances was devastating, but to be responsible, perhaps, was beyond my ability to imagine. I wouldn't have survived that guilt. But he did. I think the Manhattans helped. A lot. At least it appeared his drinking accelerated. Or maybe it was just that I noticed since my mother wasn't available to soften his inebriation. He still went to work early each morning, and on business trips, accelerating his rise through the ranks of Sears, until the multiple pitchers of Manhattans at the end of each day had some foreplay with a lunchtime toot now and again, eventually causing an early retirement. His expectations of a nightly supper, clean laundry, and weekly housecleaning remained as if Mom were dressed in her shirtwaist waiting by the three-paneled front door with cocktails and canapés. On weekends, he slept until midafternoon, a repose that initially caused me some consternation—was he, too, lying dead somewhere on the nubby carpet? And at first I would sneak into his room to see if the blankets were moving with his breath, exiting with not so much as relief but resignation, because he was coping poorly too.

His temper was short, shorter when he was loaded. In fact he had no patience. But I don't think he did before. He had effectively been shielded from the vagaries of adolescence by my mother, that's all. And while the distance between us grew even greater, it was clearly not from any strategy on his part, but from me—I stayed out of his way. I didn't try to engage him and my fractured smile deterred any comments about my attitude. I planned for the moment when I could ask about that night, after which I could safely walk away to someplace else. He was only forty-seven years old when my mother died. He was still young. I thought I had time.

The last first I counted was when I got married. It was 1970, seven years after my mother had died. I had turned twenty-one that May, with one year of college left. My father had warned me he wouldn't pay for both college costs and a wedding—my choice.

"Are you pregnant?" he snickers.

"The wedding is nine months away, Dad."

"You can't come home if this doesn't work out," he says, stabbing towards my face with his index finger.

161

I stare. Should I smile?
"I mean it," he continues somewhat alarmed that I haven't
indicated some understanding. "The door will be closed to
you. Do not, and I repeat, DO NOT come home if you have
any kind of problem."
Repetition wasn't necessary.

I don't understand fully why I persevered in planning the event (he called it off innumerable times for inane reasons), but I managed to receive enough wedding gifts to return for cash that I was able to pay my final tuition. Besides, I was determined to have as close to a traditional wedding as possible. Maybe it stemmed from my near elopement with Ray, the cherry red suitcase, and Checker Cab. Or the idealization of the event—what young female is immune to that? Perhaps I wanted a taste of normalcy, the normalcy associated with this ritual, although I suspected not every bride was intoxicated with her impending escape rather than her vows. All I know is this: after the ceremony I took my first deep breath in seven years and almost passed out from the rush of oxygen. Like my mother, I was finally safe. It was that knowledge that I wore like a wedding gown.

Little did I know then, this relationship built on predictability, respect, and loyalty would remain intact for decades. Under my husband's gaze, I was loveable, and this stirred some vestige of memory from before, when my mother most likley had locked eyes with mine. And whenever he teased that he loved me more than I did him, the secret rattled its saber, insuring my silence.

There was nothing suspicious about my motive in keeping the secret from him. I was merely protecting the image of whom he thought he had married—the funny, sarcastic, coed engineered by distance and time from her father. My resiliency rebounded or perhaps was newborn in the confinement of college. It wended itself around my spine like a brace, bolstered by the experiences I sought. When I became a dormitory resident advisor for a group of incoming freshman, an admiring father grabbed my hand and said, "I want my daughter to be just like you!" To which I stuttered a thank you at his retreating back, stifling a sob of gratitude.

Oh, the secret mattered, but not as much. And the scene from which it was spawned? I could revise it at will, although the revision never lasted long. I was still a hostage, but one with time. The last thing I would allow was a diminished adulthood, especially after tasting manna. I was determined to speak with my father. Soon.

Before the decade was out, my husband was a successful lawyer on his way to his first judgeship, two children flourished, and I taught school. Mary visited me often before she married, and later, all three of us sisters vacationed at the lake with our families, six children total, while my father worked out of the country. We hauled beach chairs to the rocky shore, and sat like our mother and her two sisters, waves lapping at our tanned thighs, laughing at irreverent remarks about life, about the idiocies of just living, accustomed to our status as the aggrieved trio. We never talked with our children about their grandmother. All we could share, really, was her death story, of which I was uncertain, and my sisters mute. So we pointed out birds, not so rare, unscrambled fishing lines, collected rocks in buckets, and sent the children off to Peanut Hill to eat peanut butter sandwiches on the lumpy cow turds. Most often, though, we caressed their little tow-headed bodies with thankful hearts, that we, the three of us, had outwitted death so far. The early childhood of our offspring was marked by laughter—that's what they remember most, that the three of us could barely catch our breath. It was hard to explain the fine line between joy and hysteria.

I rarely saw my father. He spent the first years of my marriage ignoring my existence, forgetting birthdays and holidays. I reached out on occasion, after my children were born, trying to create a grandfather from my fantasy. I asked him to be my daughter's godfather, an Irish tradition. He accepted and presented her with a sterling silver cup engraved with the wrong date of birth. The laughter that ensued was perfunctory. "Details," he said. "Big deal."

And then he got sick.

I don't remember him ever complaining of illnesses. Even as he got older, there was never any mention of his bowel movements or sore joints, except, of course, the unstoppable bleeding from his gums which led to his diagnosis of leukemia. But that was a legitimate illness, one that he didn't bring on himself unlike his drink-induced diabetes and smoker's emphysema. When he didn't go into remission right away after being wired to an IV for thirty days, he was shocked. After all, he lived with the diabetes by popping oral insulin with his first Manhattan and switched from Marlboros to Kents. I think it is notable that until the leukemia diagnosis in his early sixties, my father had never missed a day of work. Suddenly he was forced to quit a consulting job with Edgar Stores, a leading retailer of clothing and textiles in South Africa. He was going to miss his chauffeur in Johannesburg, he mused, and as usual I hoped he was hiding his grief for my sake.

Leukemia gave my father the opportunity to make some amends, to create final memories. He was dying. The chemotherapy hadn't shocked the disease into remission. With unfamiliar generosity, my father invited my sisters and me to Florida, to Sarasota, to a high-rise on the big blue Gulf. We were to bring members of our own families; we were to enjoy his final weeks. Hairless, except when he popped a pelt on his head, with a distended belly and barely tolerable hemorrhoids, my father treated us to meals and drinks, played with grandchildren, and drank moderately for the first week. It was an odd feeling. We had never had the luxury of time before death slammed against us. We watched him closely, and he talked about the hospital. I asked him if he ever saw a bright light, if he ever saw anyone familiar in his chemo dreams. He looked shocked.

"How did you know?"

I didn't have the heart to tell him I had read it in *Reader's Digest* in the hospital. But this report gave him some legitimacy.

He continued to see a physician while we were in Florida, for blood tests and comfort care, and reports on the number of rogue cells still inhabitating his bone marrow. As it turned out, he went into remission before the second week.

"What?" Patty, Mary and I screamed in unison. "Remission? You're sure?"

"It happens," my father said. "Sometimes weeks after the chemotherapy stops."

Yikes.

He got his sea legs back that second week as his liquor consumption escalated.

My father decided to lease an apartment in Sarasota after that. "I need to get on with life," he said. His two sisters and brother lived there, and if he stayed well long enough, he planned to purchase a condominium or maybe a small home. He looked forward to the future, he wanted to summer in Minnesota, winter in Sarasota, retire completely, read continuously. And drink. It only took a year for him to destroy his intestine.

The colostomy was temporary, which gave my father little solace. It interfered with his persona; he became more solitary, a little more careful, older, even though he was barely mid-sixties. But he never made one concession. When he drank beer, the colostomy bag blew up with gas and made a distressing noise, like a bleat. When he got blasted, he pumped it like a bagpipe creating the squawks in staccato. He had accidents when he forgot to empty it after his Manhattans. He should have avoided sauerkraut but didn't. He should have avoided baked beans but wouldn't. He ate corn on the cob, lima beans, and fried fish. After he was reconnected, he said he would rather die than poop into a bag again. Ironically, he did just that.

My father did find an apartment in Saint Petersburg Beach, "St. Pete's," he called it. He enjoyed the proximity to the Gulf and to his siblings. So when I heard that he just about burned the entire apartment complex to the ground, I was surprised.

"It was just a TV dinner," he told me later over the phone. "Turkey."

What he hadn't counted on during his cocktail hour that evening was tripping over his glass coffee table and fracturing his hip. But as the apartment was filling with smoke from the scorched frozen meal, he had enough sense and was sufficiently anaesthetized to crawl to the kitchen and prop himself up between the toaster oven and telephone. He called the fire department and waited for their arrival, standing in the kitchen with what I would imagine was just the right amount of machismo.

Patty, Mary, and I weren't too concerned when we heard from him, from his hospital bed in Saint Petersburg. We were pragmatic by this time. We assumed the pins that were to be inserted into his hip would hold better than his own bones. We thought the only hurdle would be negotiating the cocktail circuit with a walker. He would need a basket, we said, to carry his cocktail paraphernalia. He'll heal quickly. He's only sixty-five. He's survived worse things—colitis, leukemia, diabetes, emphysema, alcoholism—his life has been nothing but a medical overstatement. (Was there a message here, somewhere?)

Even though the surgeon determined the hip operation was a success, the declaration was a moot point. By the time my sisters and I arrived at the hospital in Florida, my father was in intensive care with a permanent colostomy, this time from peritonitis. My aunt told me it was the thought of another colostomy that did it for him. He told her from the gurney, "No way, Marge. I will not live with that bloody bag, and a walker." As it turned out, another regime of chemotherapy was in the offing as well. The leukemia decided to renew its lease. But he was never aware that he had finally struck out.

For a day or so, he raged behind his mask. Then we assembled by his bedside and Patty started to wail, "Don't die, Dad. Please don't leave us." This was 1983. Our mother had died almost exactly twenty years earlier. He had been gone for at least that long. And it occurred to me as I stood by my sister, that we had wished for this, maybe not on a shining star, but we had wished he would die before us, or at least before we lost the energy to persevere.

Patty and I never discussed how we felt trying to live around our father's irascibility all the years we were growing up. But I knew after she said in front of her girlfriends that she wished he would die, her feelings were monumentally conflicted. Of course there was an audible gasp. "How can you say that?" someone whispered. But I smiled at the back of her head as she deftly maneuvered our car in and out of driveways, dropping friends off from school, and felt less crazy. Patty's comments were as brittle as my thoughts. I had learned not to expect anyone to understand our life of secrets and inner spaces. I realized that Patty had as well. We accepted that we were different from our peers.

My sister's bedside lamentation, so many years later, struck me as something primeval. Was she trying to forestall the outcome a bit longer to give him a chance, on his deathbed, to turn into a nice man?

I noticed then the squawking of the machine settled for a moment. My father's blue eyes darted around the room. His hands were tied to the bed frame. I imagined the IV from his vein filled with truth serum. We had a chance to establish the nomenclature needed to carry on a conversation.

Should I ask? "One squawk for a 'yes' answer, two or more for a 'no.'"

(Did you kill her? Accidentally? Of course! But did you? Please make that contraption sing, one last time, for me!)

The machine rattled. It sounded like an obscenity.

"Can't the mask be slipped down for a minute?" I asked. "Just in case he has something important to say?"

I was thinking of the tawdry death scenes, the ones where final words smoothed some rotten history, the manipulative ones that made everything okay, the ones where you cried for what could have been, and then cried for what was, and ended up crying in relief. I was thinking of the scenes that ended in forgiveness. Clearly not a movie aficionado, the nurse held firm. He was going to die according to hospital protocol. He was going to die with his input and output catalogued, in his nakedness, with a new hip, a raw stoma, and three daughters looking for a sign from which to build a story. But as it turned out, on the occasion of his death, he died mum.

He died before I had the courage to ask him what happened. He died twenty years after my mother. Time had run out. How I cursed myself! My lack of courage! And my optimism! How could I have succumbed to the glass half-full image? Dammit. The secret and I were on our own.

After his death, as I began to write, I dreamt I killed my father with his hunting knife, the one he kept on his closet shelf. I happened to be looking in my toolbox that day, the one I inherited from my father, for my level. That was when I noticed the blade lying on top of everything. All I could think of was how sinister it looked. I couldn't remember how it got there, or why I had it. It must have been in the toolbox all along. So that night or shortly thereafter, I dreamt of cutting my father into a million pieces, every word another slice, hack, hack, hack, after which I stuffed him into his closet. Was I murdering the father-image my sisters had? Even though we wished him dead when he became unreasonable in his drunkenness, this was different. By dismembering my father, I was unraveling the secret and rewriting the familiar narrative of our mother's death. As I pieced the story together, would my sisters be torn apart? Was death by genetic malfunction easier to live with even if it might not be the truth?

And then it happened: the secret became the font from which anxiety, panic, and a state of hyperarousal flowed unfettered through my bloodstream. Daily noise—a glass breaking on the counter, a car horn, an ambulance siren, a slammed door, startled me. I jumped, flinched, and was visibly shaking, often shivering in fear.

"What! What is with you?" my husband would tease. "It's just the doorbell!"

But there was no dearth of adrenaline pulsing from my pancreas. Discordant piano compositions and misplaced notes undid me. Words in a certain sequence created intrusive thoughts. "Peerless Plastic Mortuary Products" from a matchbook cover unleashed a spate of poorly conceived film clips, all called, "The Wake," featuring the familiar bucketful of pink-toned preservative, too bright, too garish. (Tone her down! Pink her up! Snap that eyelid with another staple! Pin the lips together! Give her more décolletage!)

I began to smell my own adrenaline.

Our Lady of Lourdes Catholic Church sat on a sunny corner in the city, its stone edifice encroaching on a wooden door which emitted a shrill cry announcing the arrival of each celebrant to the curious congregation. If you were tardy in this church, a stylish Sunday garb was a necessity, gossip being the final prayer of the devout. Larger than a chapel, and lacking ostentation, its simplicity was soothing, especially the alcove housing the BVM, always flush with flowers matching her robe. It was here that I had my first fully formed panic attack, twenty years after my mother's death, and shortly after my father's, 1983.

It arrived *suddenly*, right at the point during the ceremony when we were instructed to offer each other some symbol of peace.

"Peace be with you," the priest says turning toward the congregation.

"Peace be with you!" most of us reply with graciousness.

And then without any guidance, the priest directs us, his flock of little lambs, to offer each other a sign of peace.

While most shake hands, a few hug, some even attempt a kiss. People turn right and left, look behind them and squeeze out from their pews, shaking and muttering, "Peace be with you. Peace. Peace. God bless. Peace. Peace. Peace." Other people hide their heads, stare straight ahead, and withhold their flesh like lepers. I knew one man who wore gloves and washed them immediately after the service. Another offered only the tips of two fingers and kept them stiffened until the end of Mass. Some even changed location if too much preening and picking was undertaken by a pew mate. Perhaps that's what caused the dizziness, I thought later.

(Scabies, ringworm, herpes, flu, colds, and pink eye, peace to you.)

This morning I was distracted by the beautiful woodwork of the pulpit, the small, rounded portico above, which looked like a cap, and the marble floor.

Who polishes all this? I wondered. And then out of nowhere, spots appeared in front of my eyes, threatening to connect themselves. My hands were shaky and clammy as I pecked my way out of the pew, whispering "peace be with you" and headed for the concrete stoop where another parishioner was having a smoke.

"I just needed some fresh air," I explained to her for no apparent reason. "I'm just a little dizzy, is all."

"Peace be with you," she said through clenched teeth as her cigarette bobbled.

It happened again when I was waiting in a line of traffic at a semaphore. Spots. Then standing in line at a grocery checkout. The line at the theatre, waiting for a table in a restaurant, lines in airports. More spots. Spots and dots accompanied by a wildly beating heart. I think I knew intuitively that if I was held too long in any one position, the secret would kill me.

My need to remain upright demanded complete attention at every turn.

"It's okay," I soothed. "You really aren't going to pass out in this line." And then I would wonder if the woman with the frozen entrees would help me. Or the boy with the acne and single box of condoms. What about the gum snapper, toe tapper, hygienically impaired? I concentrated on the floater that roamed around my eye. The little black dot darting like a pinball. I waited for a hemorrhage. I made it through to check-out.

Wiping the sweat from my face, glancing under my armpits, finding my pulse, counting missed beats, oddly these were stabilizing distractions involving movement and conscious thought. Bobbing, counting, humming, coughing. If I was in my car I opened my window and took in huge gulps of air, my mouth perfectly formed in an "o" like a fish. Sometimes I played with the clutch, lurching back and forth. I looked for escape routes. On longer trips when the freeway endlessly winged past farmland, I looked for a house in the distance and calculated the time it would take to crawl through the rows of corn to get there before my heart completely exploded. I noticed where the hospitals were in strange cities, wondered if I might die in mid-air on a plane trip, stepped carefully across heaving sidewalks, and avoided buildings that shook before my eyes. I read about vertigo and brain tumors. I wondered if I had a genetic malformation, some faulty wiring, if there was a drip, drip, drip, of blood somewhere along my venous highway.

And then, without warning, the secret leapt from my lips. It happened during an examination in a neurologist's office. I was there to see him about my right arm which had gone numb and tingly, my dizziness, and the sharp pain which stabbed at my head. In the waiting room, as I watched my pulse drumming away at the purple vein in my wrist, I was strangely calm. Maybe I had been wrong about the cause of my mother's death all along. I was her daughter after all. I was indeed having a CVA.

"So your mother died of a cerebral hemorrhage?" the doctor asked as I stood on one foot, eyes closed, pointing fingertip to nose-tip.

"I think so. I mean, yes." I wobbled enough that the doctor had to steady my arm.

"You think so?" he said shining his penlight into my cornea. He was so close I sucked in my breath. I think he did too.

"No. I didn't mean I think so," I said trying to laugh a little while I looked around for the secret. "She died of a cerebral hemorrhage, very young," I added, following his finger, right to left to center.

"Did she have bad health? Signs that you remember? Or symptoms? What did the autopsy say?"

"There wasn't an autopsy," I said, regretting this conversation. I knew I needed to just leave, make up an excuse to get out of there.

"No autopsy?" the doctor said, stopping for a moment to look at me. "When did this happen?" the doctor asked walking across the room to get my chart.

(Oh no!) "A while ago."

"How old was she?"

(Calculate.) "Uh…"

"Is there anything else?"

"Well… I think my father may have killed her."

171

(Shit, crap, damn, hell, shitcrapdamnhellshitcrapdamnhell.)

I was shaking a bit, chilled. I don't know if the doctor noticed. He seemed intent on holding his penlight steady. It was very quiet for a while in that examination room, except for the buzz of the fluorescent lights and the drumming in my head. Okay. Look normal, I admonished myself. Swing your legs, not coquettishly, of course! Don't shrug your shoulders—too dismissive. Maybe raise your eyebrows? Don't cry. Do not. You will not stop.

(Jump from the exam table and pirouette! TA-DAH.)

Maybe he hears this all the time, these utterings, like a bartender.

(Ah, pour me a Perfect Manhattan, buddy, will 'ya? Say, I think my father killed my mother. Cheers!)

"You know that's huge, don't you? HUGE," he added.

It is? I'd never thought of the secret in terms of size before. I focused on *huge* for a while, staring at the linoleum, and the black scuffs from all the doctor shoes tripping on the secrets of their patients.

"Have you ever told anyone?"

I shook my head in disbelief. The secret had become uncontrollable. I was shocked. I hadn't realized it was hanging on the very tip of my tongue ready to escape.

"We could talk, you and I," the doctor said, scribbling some notes way too fast, which I hoped would be illegible.

"Are you certain there is reason to believe your father had something to do with her death?"

"No," I whispered.

"Well, then. Perhaps it would help to sort through what you do remember."

"Not much," I said. "I actually don't remember much."

"Would you want to set a few appointments? I think it would help to talk. It might help some of your symptoms too. I did a residency in psychiatry in case you're wondering."

"Sure," I said. "That would be great." My speech was pressured. I could feel the tingling moving up my arm into my cheek. It felt hot and flushed. I gingerly touched my skin, pushing away the illusory needles pricking my flesh. I cursed myself for saying anything. I knew better. Damn the secret.

"How about this," the doctor said. "Keep track of your dreams, your daydreams for that matter, the wanderings of your mind, let's say, for a month or so, and then get back to me."

"Okay," I said. My lip twitched.

"Until then, don't worry about cerebral hemorrhages."

Hopping off the exam table, I hurried into my clothes and listened at the door for his voice. Clamping one hand over my mouth, I walked through the reception area to the parking lot and never went back.

The door had been opened and the secret wouldn't remove its foot. I teetered on the edge of confessing to my husband for months, tiptoeing around stories of casebook witnesses, picking his brain for some insight.

"Are children credible witnesses?" I ask.

"There's a debate about that," he says.

"What do you mean, a debate? Do you think children are liars?" I press.

"Some people think children can be manipulated. That their memory can be falsified," he responds.

"Oh. What would it take for a child to be taken seriously?"

I am at the sink, scrubbing furiously at something imagined, a stain that cannot be removed, from the pan, from the carpet, from me. I think of bruises invisible to the naked eye. Wounds, scabbed deep. Thick scar tissue.

"Can a child incriminate a parent?" I ask without turning around. "And evidence. Would it be admissible even if the child wasn't actually in the room when the crime occurred?"

And what about autopsies? I want to ask. Can a doctor be prosecuted for not ordering one? "What is it?" my husband asks to my back. "Is there a specific case?"

"Mine." I whisper. "I think my father may have had something to do with my mother's death."

I steady myself, waiting for the hole in the universe to gape open, an ungodly inferno ignited by my incriminating words. My stomach lurches and the trembling begins. I clamp my mouth to stop the incessant chatter, teeth striking teeth. My scalp contracts. Numbness seeps across my face, and then pins and needles as if I am about to wake from a paralysis. But I can stand. My muscles obey. The grenade that has swelled in my gut for decades diffuses. And most surprising, I can breathe.

When I turn around, my husband is still there, steadfast, concerned, helpful. His gaze is my sanctuary.

We map out a plan. How to find Dr. DeHaan.

I am teaching school. My class of seven-year-olds keeps me busy and centered. The secret remains in the supply closet with the crayons and paper and pencils until I have a minute to acknowledge its presence. I don't have time to withdraw from my life. I have commitments and responsibility. I take on as much as I can. I am running from my demon.

Time didn't heal. I went back to school and became a social worker. Time still didn't heal. My personality became disturbed. I became anxious and had somatic illnesses. I looked everything up in the Diagnostic and Statistical Manual of Mental Disorders II, a text used for determining different illnesses.

"A Panic Attack is a discrete period in which there is the sudden onset of intense apprehension, fearfulness, or terror, often associated with feelings of impending doom. Symptoms such as shortness of breath, palpitations, chest pain or discomfort, choking, or smothering sensations and fear of going crazy…"

(GOING CRAZY!)

I was all over the pages filled with anxiety symptoms. Panic Disorder, Obsessive Compulsive Disorder, Posttraumatic Stress Disorder.

(Disorderdisordedisorddisordisodisdi.)

I discovered the writings of Karen Horney in 1989. Her book on self-analysis sat on top of DSMII, the perfect antidote to the structured dissonance in my head.

She believed in this "self" process, as long as the patient had incentive. She applauded the quest for self-knowledge. She was a feminist in the era of Carl Jung and Sigmund Freud. I am certain she could spell misogynist. And she wasn't hysterical.

She didn't see women as defective and forever limited. She thought penis envy was perfectly understandable if it meant one could have power, patriarchy, and preternatural knowledge. And Womb Envy! She believed in Womb Envy for males! How I loved that. Karen was a far cry from the Pope and Pop. And patriarchy.

(Thank you, Ms. Horney. May the secret share my couch?)

The thrum of butterflies that flipped inside me, stem to stern, had served its purpose. I wanted a net to thrust them out. An exorcism. Where is a parish priest when you need one? I realized being so focused on warding off unwanted attacks of anxiousness prohibited me from remembering important information about my mother, and our interactions for thirteen years. I read about anxiety this extreme, that it was probably from irrational fears, but I couldn't convince myself that a mother suddenly here, and then not there—FOREV-ER—was rational. I mean she vanished. Poof! Like a trick of magic. For all of infinity. Ah, but how can a brain cope with infinity when it is helplessly locked in repetitive behaviors? That's good! I can't think, about IT.

Did I say I couldn't remember much about my first thirteen years? No wonder I looked in a mirror, sometimes confused as to who that was staring back with the jaundiced eye. My childhood had been erased, tabula rasa; death begat my new birth. All I had was a beat-up scrapbook. Anxiety had become my cloak of protection from the truth. I hummed to the lyrics of The Ramone's. How could a boy band get it before me?

("Nothing's right until everything is wrong. It makes no sense until I'm tense…. And I'm crazy, crazy, crazy… In a crazy world.")

It was complicated. Words like *affection* and *rejection* became intertwined with *perfectionism* and *control*. Why did I engage in the latter to such an obsessive degree? Maybe because of the former? I became confused with former and latter, right hand, left hand. I didn't know anymore.

(Bombast and bewilderment, a necrosis of the nursling, rhymes waste time.)

Always in anticipation of trouble I lay in wait. *Toujour prêt*! Be prepared! BP! My anxiety kept me at the ready. Everything was out of my control. The past, the future, mother death, and father. The secret was predictable though! Yes. It was always there. It fought for control over my anxiety. But it wasn't winning. So far. It couldn't win. Not yet. I wasn't ready. And then I remembered the book.

"To do self-analysis," Dr. Horney instructed," you must examine the details of your life, not just the highlights." Quite an exciting admonition for a perfectionist, I thought.

But I began at a highlight anyway. The cerebral hemorrhage, the cerebral vascular accident, CVA, brain to vein collision, was an insubstantial diagnosis of death, a subterfuge, enough to satisfy, but without a factual basis.

Before my thirty-seventh birthday, I had undergone an EEG, an angiogram, and MRI. The twinges in my temples continued. I had a CAT scan, my blood sugar measured, and vestigial tests. I suffered from vertigo and dizziness. Hissing radiators reminded me of my fragility. Parts of my face went numb, my hands and feet tingled. I went to the mirror and imagined I was a pincushion. The longer I stared, the more I visualized one side of my face sagging. My mother was right, I thought. My face was going to freeze into a frown. I went to a neurologist who wondered about epilepsy and an ear doctor who wondered about multiple sclerosis. I had visual acuity tests and blood drawn. I went on Dilantin. But the secret was tenacious. The more I confounded my psyche with imagined illnesses, the more attention it demanded.

My diagnoses were scattered and unsubstantiated. There was not a shred of familial history available. My mother never had an autopsy. The doctor who examined her had never done so before, unless it was between the lilac hedges separating our houses. She had no history. The only substantive medical fact I had was the red stain left on the bedroom carpet.

The audience of grandparents become attentive as I approach the microphone.

"As principal of Rowland Hall-Saint Mark's I want to welcome you to Grandparents Day." I scan the audience for someone in their late seventies. My mother. She would be seated up front with her huge smile and red lipstick. She would be proud of me. And even though I never became a pediatrician, I am keeper of the children in this little enclave of innocence and safety. I feel the tweak of the secret in my gut. I shake off the momentary dizziness which threatens my posture. I am accustomed to some disorientation by now.

"The children are waiting for your visit to their classrooms. You must know how special you are to them, and to the school. Thank you so much for spending the afternoon with us."

When I finally contacted Dr. DeHaan thirty-four years after her death—the doctor who declared my mother dead on that wintry morning, the same doctor who had to pry the phone from my paralyzed hand—and asked him about the reason for her death, about her cerebral hemorrhage, he was nothing less than shocked.

"How did you hear that? Where did that come from? Who t-t-told you that? " he stutters.

"My father," I reply.

His perplexity was palpable.

And I knew.

Chapter 10
Perfect Manhattans

Dupage County Complex. Wheaton, Illinois. A concrete morass of twelve tightly-spaced and uninspired buildings occupied several acres of land which were equipped to deal with animal care, health, juvenile detention, birth, marriage, and death. Empty glass windows looked out over parking stalls where Ford Pintos and Gremlins huddled between Oldsmobile Delta 88s, with popped hoods and lost bumpers. Picnic tables littered with cigarette butts and aluminum cans were strategically placed by a scattering of trees offering the green space of a few brown-tinged leaves. Sweat and tears cleaned their surfaces, more often than elation.

I was compelled to retrieve my mother's death certificate, if for no other reason than I had so few mementos from her life. I felt a little silly, uncertain really, as to what I would do with it. It wasn't that I needed some tangible proof of her death. After all, I had her obituary pasted in my childhood scrapbook, right by Bobby Darin. And I had the secret. But it was the only formal document available, a legal document, one authorized by an M.D., the county coroner, a deputy, the local registrar, and put on file by Lavera Kahout. It belonged to my mother. Besides, what could I glean from this scrap of paper that I didn't already know? Unless you consider the stain by the side of the bed.

(Bloody Mary, Blood Meal, the Blood of Lambs, Bloody Sorry, Blood on his hands, Beaten to a bloody stump?)

As I stood at the blue Formica counter on a sultry Tuesday in August, I ran my fingers along the graffiti scratched into the plastic and picked at the inlaid gold speckles, distracting myself from the unbearable urge to run. With what I thought was just the right amount of sobriety I said, "Hi. I would like to obtain a death certificate."

"Blue form, ma'am."

"Blue form?"

"Fill out the blue form with as much information that you have and I will locate the death certificate, provided the person died in this county, that is. I can't tell you how many people think that the place of birth will have the death certificate! Even if you lived your entire life right here, in DuPage County, but left for a short time, let's say, to go to Ohio, and died there, the certificate would be in Ohio. That will be $7.00 payable to the county clerk."

With one arm twisted out of natural proportion, the clerk tucked my completed blue form between thumb and forefinger while the other rifled through manila folders; one rubber tipped finger moving with incredible speed. What was the protocol in this type of situation, I wondered? Should I genuflect once, cross myself, sprinkle holy water over my left shoulder, bury the Infant of Prague, whisper a prayer of thanks to Saint Christopher for my safe journey, or perhaps Saint Anthony for helping to locate a lost possession?

I closed my eyes to the blur of colorful forms, white for birth certificates, yellow for marriage, until a somewhat lopsided shadow blocked the light. The death certificate, stapled to my blue form, with the receipt for $7.00 was placed in front of me.

Sitting in one of the grimy plastic chairs, I tipped my head back and counted the acoustical tiles in one row of the ceiling, and then the holes in one square, multiplied the whole lot, and forgot the numbers when I became distracted with water stains zigzagging across the width of the room. I watched the young couples applying for marriage licenses, fidgety and embarrassed as if we all could see into their marriage-bed minds. I heard couples dropping the names of foreign places a little too loudly as they signed for their passports and saw birth certificates notarized for legitimacy.

It occurred to me as I unfolded the death certificate of my mother, that she had been dead longer than she had been alive. Dizziness and nausea swept over me as I noted the condensed information about her. It didn't take long. There wasn't much. And anyway, it was Line 18 that interested me. The line that listed cerebral hemorrhage as the cause of death. Maybe I *should* just accept it, this diagnosis of death, as written by the authorities, the professionals, the medical personnel that knew how to determine those causes that occur suddenly and unexpectedly, like a flash, before one could say *Jack Robinson!* And without an autopsy. Yes. Accept and desist, I prayed to myself.

But before I reached *Amen,* I reached Line 18 and cerebral hemorrhage was not printed there or anywhere. I sucked all the air out of the room as my brain defaulted for a moment to Dr. Seuss and his inane rhymes.

(From there to here and here to there, funny things are everywhere.)

And the secret? It sat on my chest, its voracious appetite appeased for the moment.

NAME OF DECEASED was listed as Dorothy Donnelly, instead of Dorothy Jean. Even the initial "J" was omitted, although there was a place, a small space.

(This left me with an aftertaste, as my brain wrapped itself around the word haste.)

It was just Dorothy, on Line 3, without the Jean and Josephine, the last name selected when she was eleven and received the sacrament of Confirmation.

Line 17, Informant Signature, was filled with the typed name of my father, Thomas C.—a middle initial! But, where was he, the signatory?

(He couldn't sign, I thought with dread. His hands were paralyzed with fear instead.)

Line 21 a, Accident, Suicide, Homicide or Undetermined—a choice was never made. "Neither" filled the box.

(Neither this nor neither that, neither here nor there; neither fish, flesh or fowl, but perhaps mon pere…)

The year was wrong, the year that the certificate was filed. It was off by 365 days. Not after but before; 1962 instead of '63. Line 25 put my brain in overdrive. I pressed the document to my ear, turning it backwards like a Beatle's Album.

(Does the blackbird sing in the dead of night? Is Paul dead while Dot's on the lam? The death certificate was as suspected, a complete, unholy sham.)

There were no signatures on the Certificate of Death. Not one. Nothing was scrawled—illegible or indecipherable—from any of the major players. The County Coroner, the Funeral Director, the Local Registrar—even the Doctor that declared her dead—hadn't touched pen to paper.

(The certificate was remarkable, as you can see, in its errors of fact, and illegitimacy.)

Line14 on the Coroner's Certificate of Death, where Mother's Full Maiden Name was to be entered, it said Florine Kost instead of Florine Theresia Kost with 'Mups' in parenthesis. (Minor, to be sure, but it's the minors that make up a life.)

In box Number 20 on the Coroner's Certificate of Death, an 'x' marked "No Autopsy".

I couldn't find a coroner or doctor who denied that this death was undoubtedly one for an investigation. The suddenness of her death required an autopsy by Illinois law unless she had recently been under the care of a physician for at least one of her death diagnoses.

(Headaches or a heart ailment or a womb dismemberment, the next diagnosis for sure.)

How was my mother disqualified for her rightful place on the autopsy table? She was thirty-seven years old, hadn't seen a doctor since the birth of Mary, died alone in her bedroom, leaving behind a stain by the side of the bed and three traumatized children. If anyone deserved the Y cut, it was my mother.

As my eyes continued to shred the document they stopped, riveted, next to Question 18, Cause of Death. It read Coronary Occlusion.

Huh?

(Damn, I thought. A heart attack? I knew I should have had an EKG.)

By the time I located the doctor who had pronounced my mother dead, he had lost an arm, become a psychiatrist, moved from the neighborhood, and grown old. I wondered if his hair was thick and gray, if he was still attractive and well dressed, if his wife, Marilyn, continued to display her hundreds of lipsticks on her vanity, tube after tube of wonderful colors which I lavished on myself during my years of babysitting.

The death certificate was lying on my kitchen counter as I listened to the phone ringing into a space I could only imagine. Line 18, entitled, Medical Cause of Death, Coronary Occlusion, swam in front of my eyes. My palm was sweaty, my breath shallow. I held the phone tight to my ear and lay down on the cool tile.

"Do you remember me, Dr. DeHaan? After all these years? We lived next door. I tended your children. How are they?" A nervous twitch played up and down my ribcage in staccato.

Guardedly, he said, "Fine." And it occurred to me that as a psychiatrist, he might be opening his DSM IV Manual for a diagnosis, his Mont Blanc held mid-air, until it gradually descended to his empty shirtsleeve for a refined scratch, perhaps to soothe an illusory itchiness that arose when anxious. I tried to be upbeat, and matter of fact. I didn't want to alarm him before retrieving whatever information he might have. His voice was familiar, the Chicago accent intact. Soothing. I imagined his patients readily engaged in their life perils in his presence.

"Of course, I remember you and your family," he continued. "Your mother's death was a significant event for me. Such a tragedy."

"I was visiting my sisters in Chicago last week. We had a great time! They are doing really well. We all married wonderful men," I said for some reason, the stiffness in my voice like an old arthritic limb unused to this arduous task.

"I visited our neighborhood. Hawthorne Boulevard. Our house looks great. The trees have grown."

(The grass is green. Zinnias gold. Sidewalks lined with lies so bold.)

"Still the same white paint and black shutters."

I didn't tell him I looked for the break in the lilac hedge where he slipped through, his house to ours, that early morning in January.

"Mary, my sister, and I decided to get our mother's death certificate." I pictured his pen blinking a red light. Danger. "I don't really know why. We were surprised at what was written on it."

"What do you mean?" he said haltingly.

"Instead of it saying she died of a cerebral hemorrhage…"

"Wait!" Dr. Dehaan cut in. "How did you hear that? Where did that come from? Who t-t-told you that?"

"My father, of course. The entire family always said her death was due to a cerebral hemorrhage. My grandfather recorded it as the cause of death in his family history. He gave us all a copy. All over town there were stories about her behavior at the restaurant that night. That she wasn't behaving normally, that maybe she had a migraine. Even the residents around Big Fish Lake where we vacationed each summer talked about it. My sisters and I were warned that this type of accident could have genetic links, that we needed to be wary. We were very careful, I should add. We each had CT scans of our brains when we turned thirty-seven, complete neurological work-ups. We even avoided certain medications."

I didn't tell him how our medical histories were premised on this medical anomaly—cerebral hemorrhage—since we were children. Or that every year that I lived beyond thirty-seven, the age she died, felt like a bonus year. I didn't mention that sometimes I even pleaded with God to give me just this one last Christmas, or summer vacation, or one more year.

"But she didn't die of a cerebral hemorrhage," said Dr. DeHaan, cutting into my disquieted mind.

"I know," I said. "That's why I'm calling you. I couldn't believe the death certificate said coronary occlusion. A heart attack! After all these years…"

"Wait!" Dr. Dehaan broke in again. "I don't understand. A heart attack is listed on the death certificate?"

"Yes," I said shaking uncontrollably. "It says coronary occlusion."

"May I call you back?" said the Doctor.

Could it be—a third diagnosis of death awaited me? Stop, look, listen; father, son and holy ghost; lock, stock, and barrel; three bears; three pigs; three blind mice; blood, sweat, tears; hook, line, sinker; three billy goats gruff; three men in a tub; morning, noon, night; three Musketeers; cool, calm, collected; three course meal; three bean salad; the trinity, a triptych; shamrock; the Sanctus; three cheers; three guesses; three knocks; three wishes; mother, father and Perfect Manhattan; love, honor, obey; dura mater, arachnoid, pia mater; fiddler's three; snap, crackle, pop; id, ego, superego; Tom, Dick and Harry; past, present, future; three stooges; perfect measurements—36, 24, 36; A B C and 1 2 3 times a charm; beginning, middle, end—death comes in threes.

In the world of medical examiners, there are five possible causes of death—homicide, suicide, accident, natural, or unknown, the latter when the examiner cannot determine the manner in which a person died. When I think about it, all but natural causes could have fit the bill.

If she had been granted an autopsy, we would know the contents of her stomach, or perhaps her intestine, putting the menu of the Carousel under the harshest scrutiny. (Don't order the veal chops, the headline might read!) And her brain would have been weighed and sliced and diced, and her heart the same, except the coronary arteries would have been examined, for sure, especially with the diagnosis of coronary occlusion peeking aggressively over the horizon. And the stain she left behind? Her final exhalation? Wouldn't that be worthy of its own autopsy? But it seems nothing amiss would have been found, so far, at least, according to Doctor DeHaan, the man who declared her dead. What *did* he see?

The next time the Dr. called, I had already decided to disengage myself from any further parallel play. I had to be direct, unemotional, and detached. (How many times can one be propelled through the stages of grieving before it becomes redundant! She's dead, for God's sake. Be angry over the lie, my brain shrieked in the background.)

My posture was rigid. My knees were locked into position, sphincter tight, stomach clenched. I clutched the receiver to my ear and cleared my throat. My hands were wet. My mouth was dry.

(It must be gravity which pulls the moisture from the salivary glands, rerouting the moisture to the extremities in times of fear. Where is my spittle? Fiddle. Middle. Riddle. Scadiddle.)

"I drove by the neighborhood the other day," Dr. Dehaan began. "My old house, unlike yours, looks a little worse for wear. The paint is peeling and the yard looks overgrown, especially the lilac hedge. Anyway, I picked up a copy of the death certificate as well—the death certificate of your mother. I wanted to see what signatures were on it. I couldn't remember if I had signed it."

"There weren't any signatures," I whispered.

"Well, that wasn't unusual in those days. I mean people weren't so suspicious back then."

"Suspicious?" I said, pinching my arm, suddenly feeling chastised.

"I realize everyone wants to make sense of their life," Dr. De-Haan said defensively. "But really, your parents weren't so bad."

(Stay on track. I pinched my arm again. And again.)

"Not, my life," I interrupted. "My mother's life. I want to make sense of her life. And if my father had something to…" I couldn't finish the sentence. My brain was unraveling. I pictured my gray matter lying in straight lines on the tile disconnecting words from their linear route—brain to voice—reason to articulation.

But only silence followed. Dr. DeHaan must be having the same problem, I thought.

I felt sleepy, lethargic. For a moment I thought I had actually slipped away. I tried to remain calm. I didn't want to scare him away. But was nonchalance possible? I cleared my throat at the same moment Dr. DeHaan cleared his. I tried not to eavesdrop on my mind. But it was impossible.

(Let's synchronize our swim, tiptoe through the tulips, skip to my Lou.)

"It wasn't a coronary occlusion," he stammered. "She didn't die of a heart attack."

(May I take a minute, Doctor, and grieve once more? I have two diagnoses and a third to score.)

How should I respond without sounding glib?

"Oh, the death certificate is wrong too?"

"No problem."

"No big deal."

"Whatever."

"Dead is dead."

"Then what was it?" I said quickly before I lost my nerve. "What did my mother die of?"

I was hunched over by now, my head between my knees, gasping for air. My teeth rattled under a blitzkrieg of shaking.

"She was asphyxiated," Dr. DeHaan said just as quietly.

(By gas, a pillow, a Halloween mask, a sock, some tape, my father's silver flask?)

"Asphyxiation?" I stuttered again, buying some time. "*Asphyxiation?*"

"Suffocation. She had too much to drink that night. I don't know how to say this but she died in her own vomit."

(Ah, the Perfect Manhattan.)

I stood up. The receiver remained by my ear, yet I couldn't feel my hand. In a way I wanted to disconnect. My bravery coagulated in a lump which I tried to swallow. The image of my mother as pure; the image of my mother as the victim; the image of my mother as protectoress; vanished.

"Let me understand this then," I said through my rattling teeth. "She didn't die of a cerebral hemorrhage, correct?"

"No. But like I said before, I never heard of that story before you told me."

"And the diagnosis of coronary occlusion that is on her death certificate is wrong, too?

"Yes. But that wasn't unusual. Coronary occlusion was used as a diagnosis of death when the real cause would do nothing constructive. I mean putting down asphyxiation would have done more harm to your family. It was a tragedy. And then that? So someone put down heart attack to suspend any future inquiry."

But someone had to tell the coroner what to put down, I thought. Or perhaps it was simply a clerical function, a phone call, physician to county filer, LaVera Kahout.

(Remember, people weren't so suspicious in those days!)

"Your father felt guilty enough. Everyone needed to get on with their lives."

(UnattendedAloneMessyMasticatedMaraschinosPartyClothesAlcoholRelatedDeathSuddenlySearsExecutiveDistinguishedlyDistraughtThreeGirlsProtectPreserveMotherImageAlcoholOverdoseVomitStainTerribleAccident. Guilty. Father felt so guilty. V-O-M-I-T! Ah, the truth of an autopsy could prove embarrassing. It was the nemesis of the emesis. Besides, WE ALL HAD TO GET ON WITH OUR LIVES, he said.

"Did you say vomit, Doctor? She died in her own vomit?"

I stood by a window, looking through my backyard into a canyon. It was impossible to see its depth from this vantage point. I felt strange as if I were positioned over a precipice. I can either fall or fly, I imagined.

(Your father felt guilty enough.)

"You know, Dr. DeHaan," I said. "I have to ask you one more thing. I always wondered if my father, well you know, might have gotten angry. After all I heard something that night."

(Please ask me what I heard. Please.) "And I wondered if perhaps he had..." (Knocked, hit, dropped, smacked, struck, whacked, kicked...yes... that's it...)

"Kicked her in the head."

"Doctor?"

"Are you still there?"

"Like I said before, we all try to make sense of our lives."

And then he hung up the phone.

I read later that coronary occlusion accounts for over seventy-five percent of all diagnoses of sudden deaths handled by medical examiner's offices. Even in suspicious or violent deaths, examiners will attribute coronary disease as a contributor to the death—maybe not first-line, but there. And besides, coronary occlusion doesn't take up much room on the death certificate; it is neat and tidy and, it would seem, at the ready to keep the lid from blowing off the truth. It is the quintessential white lie.

(After all, wouldn't all of us have a little artery hardening after a meal at the Carousel Restaurant?)

The last time I went to the lake, I stayed in the A-frame my father had constructed in the gully. I imagined it sizzling on the smoldering embers of the lifetime of bonfires that burned beneath its foundation. It was an open floor plan with a conversation pit, one enclosed bedroom, and a small septic system which we managed to uncork every time our families converged on the place en masse. My father built it as a vacation home for family, although it really only comfortably accommodated him. My grandparents' cottage had been sold, my grandfather's outbuildings mostly torn down, and the fence made of intertwining logs (crazy old man) gone. The huge windows which were latched to the ceiling most of the summer had been replaced. My parents' cottage and barn had been purchased by my mother's brother—an unwelcome neighbor to be sure, but my father didn't quibble when it came to cold hard cash for the place. It was painted a fiery hell red, as was the barn. The garbage pit was thankfully filled with soil and civilized cans with snap-on lids were located on a cement pad. The road was paved (paved!) behind the cottages, and I could only smile at the stealth with which Patty and I could have slipped the Brown Bomber onto its surface for our forays into the hinterlands of our teen-age debauchery. Peanut Hill was flanked by cottages, big houses that were all-season now, although farmers still used the hillside for grazing cows. I imagined the paddies were plentiful, although I didn't check. El Rancho was a campground, "from tents to RV's," and still offered horseback riding. The old farmhouse had been demolished. I walked the outline of the foundation that summer, looking for memories of the farm mother, the mother that left me bereft by her disappearance each summer, even though she was a figment of my imagination. All that remained were a few determined rose bushes heavy with bloom growing in the wake of the outhouse. The public beach was swarmed with a new crop of chiseled young men and families with tanned children. The downturn in vocations left the Benedictine convent sparsely populated, El-Dick's had closed, and fishermen used expensive fake bait.

The BVM retained her place on the altar by the road, wildflowers surrounded the granite kneeler, votive candles coated with mosquitoes and flies remained unlit, a rosary was placed deliberately, it seemed, by her sandaled feet. Cobwebs cloaked the statue, a gauzy veil which I swiped at with a broom, hoping the new owners of my grandparent's cottage wouldn't mind. And then I knelt on the hard slab and thought of the cerebral hemorrhage, the coronary occlusion, the asphyxiation. I thought of my mother's life and death with profound uncertainty. The only thing I knew for certain was the secret.

I walked down the twenty-six steps to the dock and lay in the water looking skyward, willing the lake gods to release their grip. Once again I felt the cool water rush over my body, and as I turned my face towards the lake bottom, eyes wide open, I saw the sunlight as it bounced across the rocky bottom leading me to shore.

I tried one last time contacting Dr. DeHaan. His office had been leased to a gynecologist— strange transition to be sure.

(Please lie in these stirrups and tell me your story!)

He left no forwarding address. Had he allowed his APA Membership to lapse? Completed his practice? Felt satisfied as he reflected on the history of his life? I searched and couldn't find him. If he were alive, I wondered if he thought of me, and my mother; if he reflected much on that night and the ramifications of his conceit to alter the truth.

I wondered if he questioned that within the ambiguity of her death resided many unappealing scenarios.

Did she have a cerebral hemorrhage and vomit? Or a coronary

occlusion causing some retching, and thus the stain? Are these accounts seamlessly woven together? She was helpless and remained on the floor of the bedroom where my father dropped her unceremoniously ("How could you embarrass me like that?") thus causing a brain injury, followed by vomiting, thus taxing her heart. Or she was drunk, plain and simple, the Perfect Manhattan becoming imperfect as it was spewed into the carpet where she lie unable to move herself, unable to turn just a bit, unable to save herself. Her fault. (This final hypothesis, however, has little evidence. I do not remember my mother ever being drunk. And if she were so horribly incapacitated, why would my father affirmatively abandon her as he slept in the living room? To teach her a lesson? "Oh you'll pay for this in spades, Dot!")

And then I remind myself of the facts.

The family myth of sudden death by cerebral hemorrhage was propagated by my father. Dr. DeHaan had no knowledge of this conclusion. The death certificate listing coronary occlusion was in error, disputed by Dr. DeHaan as well. And while her asphyxiation was the final pronouncement, what about what I saw that night? Her body dragged up the hallway. And what I heard, "Don't hurt me." My father's lament, "How could you embarrass me like that?" What about the silence of the doctor when I asked if she had been hurt in some way? By my father. (Oh so hard to ask). And his response, "We all try to make sense of our lives." Why this vagueness? Why not refute my question with evidence from his examination of her? Why not end my speculation?

So I am left with what I know. What I always knew.

I keep thinking my grieving will run out, that somehow it can be fixed, with a few pills, or a plaster cast, certainly more than a Band-Aid. But of course, it only mutates in synchronicity with my life and rears its head at unexpected times, *suddenly*, distracting me for a moment with profound loneliness. Yet, it is at those times that I will remember my mother and know that the love I am capable of giving came from her. Where else would I have learned this generosity?

She was my role model, if only for a brief time, and sometimes when I see myself in perfect stride with my own children, I see her with me.

Epilogue

A Reverie

I sit opposite Perry Mason, an expanse of polished wood separating us. Sun lays its tracks on thick wool carpet, deep brown, the color of his eyes. Even an adolescent like myself is subsumed by the depth of his eye color. One thick, perfectly coiffed brow is raised expectantly. It is soothing that he has that much control.

I think that if my story is to be told, why not to him who has a reputation of solving every case except for one, "The Witless Witness"? I pinch myself hard for distraction; to stay on track and not replay that episode in my mind. Della, Mr. Mason's assistant, hovers briefly in the doorway and vanishes. They must have a secret code.

I tell him what I heard that night, what I saw and what I did, which wasn't enough to save my mother's life. (*Twist the knob, dammit.*) I tell him my father was embarrassed. I heard him actually say, "How could you embarrass me like that. In front of my business partners." It wasn't a stretch to imagine he was angry as well. He did get angry. You learned early on not to cross him.

I didn't know if she had a thunderclap headache, the type that warns of an impending brain bleed. Or if she was confused. But yes, she was nauseous. There was a stain by the side of the bed. And remember Dr. DeHaan said she vomited? She suffocated in the mess of her emesis.

I heard her say, "Don't hurt me," to the only other person in the room that night. My father. Was there some sort of trauma? Be-

193

ing dropped? A kick? A drop-kick? Causing a brain bleed? And, re-member, it was my father who made the diagnosis of death, cerebral hemorrhage. There was no autopsy. How did he know it was a CVA? Dr. DeHaan didn't even have that information.

I tell Mr. Mason that I had been reading about murder and man-slaughter and not meaning to kill someone but it happening or meaning to kill someone on purpose or actually plotting someone's demise which is the worst. It seems, the question is, if my mother were left on the floor, drunk, very drunk, or in the throes of a brain bleed, was it neglectful that my father did not check on her or stay with her? The law seems to focus on reasonable people and what they would do. I guess a reasonable person wouldn't leave a spouse of almost fifteen years alone if she were that drunk.

Mr. Mason nods and admits it could be manslaughter, yes, invol-untary, of course. He has had plenty of cases in his career involving unintended consequences of misadventures like this. I think he was surprised by my grasp of the law, as young as I was. But then, he has no idea of how my mother's death consumed my life.

Almost anyone is capable of a crime under certain circumstanc-es, he said. What I always look for in these cases sounds simple but isn't really. We want to know what caused the death. Was it a cerebral hemorrhage or alcohol or a violent act? I would want to find out what the actual event was; if it was a brain bleed, did that occur genetically or by some other force? If she was inebriated, was she vulnerable lying on the floor unattended? You can see how difficult it is to legally classify these things.

Yes, I told Mr. Mason. I see the difficulty. But can you figure it out? How she died? Is there some way to find the evidence? That is all I want.

Not without involving your father, Mr. Mason says. And your two sisters. Probably your Aunt Shirley, the one airing the dirty laundry. And Dr. DeHaan would be very important. The business associates they had dinner with the night in question. Perhaps the servers at The Carousel Restaurant. Neighbors, perhaps. Had they ever heard arguments coming from your home on Hawthorne Blvd.? Maybe your grandparents, Mups and Gramps, you call them? All that time spent at Big Fish Lake together. It would be nice to be able to call the parish priest who heard your father's confession that morning. But, obviously, that is privileged. Maybe the coroner. Why didn't he order an autopsy? After all, it was the law in Illinois for an unattended death of someone so young. Was he convinced somehow not to do one? Oh and the funeral home, Kampp and Sons. Even your mother's long-time hairdresser, John, wasn't it? He was called to the funeral home during those days of the Wake. Maybe over the years your mother confided in him. Speaking of confidantes, friends. The Fuller Brush Man? The cleaning lady? Even Aunt Wee Wee…

And me, I whisper, interrupting him.

Yes, Perry Mason says. You are the only one who can open the door.

Acknowledgements

My bookshelves overflow with the work of brave memoir writers from whom I learned the craft, an education rivaling any MFA. My first reader, Mike, thank you for wading through the first draft with Carl Jung, Sigmund Freud, and Karen Horney. You always believed the story was compelling. Kristi, my dear friend, your encouragement, questions and suggestions continue to be invaluable as you so graciously peruse my writing from memoir to poetry. My son, Michael, your compilation of a playlist was the perfect accompaniment to *The Coroner's Lie*, from draft to draft. To my sister, Patty, thank you for your validation. I know the book was hard to read. And Joann, your technical assistance was appreciated beyond measure. Lastly, Dorothy Jean, you have been missed.

About the Author

Mickey Murphy was born in Chicago, Illinois, and grew up in the suburb of Wheaton spending most summers on Big Fish Lake in Minnesota. She has worked extensively in the field of education, teaching elementary school students, as principal of an elementary school, and as a clinical instructor at The University of Utah where she taught literacy and ran the Early Childhood Program and at Westminster College where she taught literacy. She has worked with autistic children in a clinical setting, was a juvenile probation officer and a crisis worker in a children's hospital. She holds a master's degree in social work, as well as a BA in elementary education. In addition to writing "The Coroner's Lie", the author is working on a book about meth addiction as well as a book of poetry. The author also works in multi-media, primarily Polaroid transfers and collage. She is an amateur classical pianist, perfecting most of the Bach Inventions during the pandemic. She is married with two adult children and lives in Wellesley, MA.